homegrown berries

WITHDRAWN

homegrown BERRIES

Successfully Grow Your Own
Strawberries, Raspberries,
Blueberries, Blackberries,
and More

TIMBER PRESS
PORTLAND ■ LONDON

Revised and expanded by Teri Dunn Chace.

New and revised material copyright © 2014 by Timber Press, Inc. All rights reserved.

This work incorporates portions of *The Berry Grower's Companion* copyright © 2000 by Barbara L. Bowling.

Frontispiece by Marci LeBrun
Illustrations by Kate Francis
Lettering by Patrick Barber

Published in 2014 by Timber Press, Inc.

The Haseltine Building
133 S.W. Second Avenue, Suite 450
Portland, Oregon 97204-3527
timberpress.com

6a Lonsdale Road
London NW6 6RD
timberpress.co.uk

Cover design by Breanna Goodrow
Text design by Patrick Barber
Printed in China

Library of Congress Cataloging-in-Publication Data

Homegrown berries: successfully grow your own strawberries, raspberries, blueberries, blackberries, and more.—First edition.
    pages cm
  Other title: Successfully grow your own strawberries, raspberries, blueberries, blackberries, and more
  Includes index.
  "This work incorporates portions of The Berry Grower's Companion copyright ©2000 by Barbara L. Bowling."
  ISBN 978-1-60469-317-1
  1. Berries. 2. Ornamental berries. I. Bowling, Barbara L. The berry grower's companion. II. Title. III.
  Title: Successfully grow your own strawberries, raspberries, blueberries, blackberries, and more.
  SB381.D86 2014
  634'.7—dc23

                                                2014009483

contents

Introduction: You Can Do It! 6

BERRY BASICS 11

BERRIES IN YOUR YARD 35

STRAWBERRIES 51

RASPBERRIES AND BLACKBERRIES 85

BLUEBERRIES 125

SPECIALTY BERRIES 155

Recommended Cultivars by Region 190

Further Reading and Resources 196

Acknowledgments 198

Photography Credits 199

Index 201

INTRODUCTION: YOU CAN DO IT!

Whether you are new to gardening berries, or new to gardening altogether, this book will help you welcome tasty, healthful, beautiful berries to the world that lies just beyond your doorstep. Just one homegrown berry, plucked on the way from drive to doorbell, can bestow a dizzying flavor profile, from sweet to tart to simply divine, and the ways to incorporate berries into the landscape can be similarly satisfying and diverse. Perhaps it'll be as subtle as a delicate edging of strawberries along the path leading up to your front stoop. Or maybe it'll be a bigger story, like a row of plump blueberry bushes or a property-defining fence, covered in trailing blackberries.

Raising berry crops on a small scale not only yields a tasty harvest, it makes an attractive scene. If you don't have a lot of space, choose more compact-growing cultivars and plant fewer plants.

What is a berry exactly? To botanists, a berry is a fruit that is multiseeded and derived from a single ovary. So, before we embark on this berry-growing journey, a confession: some of the fruits in this book (blueberries, currants, gooseberries, elderberries) *are* true berries; others (strawberries, raspberries, blackberries, Juneberries) are not. But for the purposes of this book, the common term "berries" will be employed for all. More important than terms, of course, are the joy, satisfaction, and delicious harvests your plantings will provide for seasons to come.

The basic concept of growing berries is hardly revolutionary—this diverse group of fruits has been a source of sustenance throughout history—but the ornamental value of berries in the landscape is increasingly recognized and celebrated. It's entirely doable to have a good-looking display that also feeds you and your family. Growth habits of berry plants range from groundcovers (strawberries) to vines that require support (trailing blackberries) to upright, freestanding shrubs (highbush blueberries). Any of these can become a significant part of your

Ripe blueberries are easy and fun to pick. Your main competition will be from birds—which can be kept away by netting until it's time to harvest.

home landscape, as productive as a good vegetable garden or small home orchard and, with savvy siting and good care, no less attractive. If your yard space is at a premium, a collection of containers is a viable planting option for most of the berries in this book. And the ever-growing abundance of available cultivars means gardeners don't have to choose between the delicious, beautiful, and disease-resistant attributes of a plant. We can have it all—an edible, natural-looking landscape that requires minimal maintenance once established.

So, how to decide which berries are a good fit for you? Berry by berry, the chapters in this book will walk you through the best selections for home cultivation. You may choose to grow exotic-sounding elderberries or black currants simply because they are impossible to find at your local grocery

WHEN DO YOU WANT THEM?

Berries ripen from spring to fall. Some are ready in early summer, some color and sweeten up later in the season; a few go all summer long, once established. Also, within any one type, different cultivars ripen at different times, allowing you either to tailor the timing of the harvest to your climate and preferences, or to grow a few different cultivars in order to extend your picking season.

Ripening-season information (ranging from very early to mid to very late) will be listed with each recommended cultivar in the lists in the individual chapters. Make sure to study these lists with care, and crosscheck with local experts and your nursery source if you need help deciding. Here's the general picture, however:

Spring to midsummer: June-bearing strawberries, black raspberries, June-berries, gooseberries, red currants, white currants.

Midsummer: red raspberries, purple raspberries, most blueberries, black currants, jostaberries.

Late summer into fall: fall-bearing red raspberries, fall-bearing blackberries, some blueberries (including rabbit-eyes), elderberries, huckleberries, chokeberries, cranberries, lingon-berries.

All summer (or on-and-off all summer): alpine strawberries, day-neutral strawberries.

Early summer and again in late summer or fall: everbearing strawberries, blackberries.

A three-season bounty of homegrown berries can be yours. Plant ones you've always wanted, but save a spot or two for ones you are less familiar with—you might be pleasantly surprised.

store. Or perhaps you'll be drawn to the basics that fill your berry fantasies all winter long: ruby-red strawberries, juicy blackberries, succulent blueberries. But keep in mind that even if they look visually familiar, your homegrown berries will almost certainly taste far superior to their mass-produced relatives. Because many berries are picked very firm, before they are ripe, to survive shipping and extend their short shelf life, those found on grocery shelves are often a bland, expensive disappointment. Fresh berries grown in your backyard, by contrast, will inspire comment—"Oh my, this raspberry tastes like a *raspberry*." No fancy descriptors needed.

This remarkable assortment of shapes, sizes, and flavors is also astoundingly good for you. Berries are high in nutrition and fiber, low in fat, and often contain impressive levels of numerous healthful compounds. To complement these natural health benefits, the methods described in this book will give

MORE REASONS TO GET GROWING

Never grown edible berries before? Thinking it's high time to try? This short list of general encouragement should inspire confidence.

• Like vegetable gardening, you get to enjoy an edible harvest. Like many favorite vegetable crops, well-sited, well-planted berry plants are vigorous and gratifyingly productive.

• Unlike many tree fruits, berry plants produce early in their life span and don't absolutely require pollinizers, complicated spraying programs, and tedious annual thinning of individual immature fruits. Also, they take up less space.

• Raising berries is not that different from growing many common flowers or shrubs—the plants are attractive, sometimes in three seasons; they too bring color, and they may be fragrant.

• Berry plants are perennials. That is, you do not have to replant them every year.

• Culturally speaking, berry plants are pretty easy to please. And just as easy are the steps you can take to mitigate any disease or pest issues you may encounter—please read on.

Pride and joy—imagine how delicious your own just-picked, sun-kissed homegrown berries will be!

you all the tools you'll need to grow your own berries without resorting to pesticides and other garden chemicals, which home gardeners increasingly—and naturally—want to avoid.

Like growing vegetables, the process of gardening berries is contagiously exciting and is something for the whole family to enjoy. Kids will delight in locating the season's first strawberry, hidden underneath a thick canopy of foliage, or filling a container with as many smoothly cool blueberries as they can reach.

So plant your berries for any number of reasons: an edible approach to beautifying and defining your outdoor space, a legitimate excuse for wandering the garden on a clear June morning, or a way to inspire random acts of strawberry shortcake and blueberry cobbler. The myriad ways to enjoy your berry harvest run the gamut from fresh to processed, savory to sweet. You aren't likely to need much help in the methods-of-consumption department; you will, however, need the practical information in this book to get from here to there. So what are we waiting for? Let's get those berry plants out of your dreams and into the ground.

berry basics

ALL BERRIES DISCUSSED IN THIS BOOK

are flowering perennials, and (with the exception of the strawberry) all are woody. Their perennial nature is important and can be used to the gardener's advantage (you can look forward to crops for years, or even decades, to come), not to mention that the very sight of them in different seasons is a pleasure to behold—think fiery red blueberry foliage holding strong, long after the last berry has been enjoyed, or the frothy white flowers of elderberries greeting you on a sunny summer day. Maintaining any berry planting requires vigilant care that includes preventing pests and attending to routine tasks such as pruning and weed removal. A little good luck doesn't hurt either.

Even perennials need a little help. Choose an appropriate cultivar, give your plants the space, care, and support they need to thrive, and reap the rewards for years to come.

From site selection to disease prevention, this chapter gives an overview of the essential steps for successful berry cultivation. As with vegetables, growing berries requires us to get outside, walk amid the plants, inspect for trouble, prune, and touch the leaves. The importance of careful, timely management based on close, hands-on observation and attention to detail cannot be overstated. Visit your plants!

Before launching into the world of berry growing, heed one important caveat: the berry crops discussed in this book are all, albeit to varying degrees, quite sensitive to local growing conditions. Make sure to consult with other growers in your area and with your local Cooperative Extension Service office to learn more about growing berries in your particular location.

LOCATION, LOCATION, LOCATION

Realtors always say that the three most important factors affecting a property's value are location, location, and location. The same goes for selecting a site for your berry patch. Location—of three sorts—is key. Where do you intend to plant your future delectables?

Macroclimate

The first location (and a primary concern) is your large-scale macroclimate, or USDA (United States Department of Agriculture) hardiness zone. If you are able to choose where you live based on where raspberries grow best, you are one lucky gardener. But if you are like most of us, you're already rooted somewhere and have to work within

NIPPING FROST DAMAGE IN THE BUD

A concern for some berry gardeners is that the flower buds or young flowers will get damaged by a late frost. Cold weather also inhibits pollinating insects, including bees. When this happens, your crop is reduced or even ruined.

The easiest way to avoid this problem, especially if you live where cold weather lingers in the spring, is to choose later-flowering varieties and/or short-season ones that can still produce in your climate.

Any time an unwelcome cold snap is forecast, though—mid to late spring—simply go out to your plants and cover them before the sun goes down and the temperature drops. Use row covers or even old blankets.

Berry plants are perennials, and some are better than others at withstanding cold. So always check before buying that the ones you want can tolerate your winters.

the constraints of your zone. You first need to find out if it is even possible to produce a particular berry in your current location. In many cases you may be able to grow certain cultivars of a plant but not others. For example, gardeners in the Pacific Northwest can grow 'Tulameen' and 'Willamette' raspberries; move to central Pennsylvania, however, and those cultivars will not make it through the first winter—whereas 'Canby' raspberries will thrive. This book provides some general information on cultivar selection within each type of berry, but be sure to check out local sources for information on what grows best in your location. (Please also consult the lists at the back of this book for a summary of recommendations by region.)

Because the ability of a given plant to survive in a particular location is so often limited by its ability to withstand cold temperatures, a word about hardiness is in order.

Throughout this book you will find discussions of the relative hardiness of cultivars for each berry. These refer to how well a plant withstands winter temperatures when completely dormant—but this is not a perfect system.

In addition, some plants may lose dormancy more quickly (meaning they require less chilling) than others as winter drags on. Once they have lost some of that dormancy, the plants are more active metabolically (even though they still *look* dormant) and may be injured at considerably higher temperatures than that at which they were completely dormant. Furthermore, typical hardiness ratings do not take into account injury from frosts in the spring.

View hardiness ratings as guides, therefore, not absolute measures. It's tempting to be adventuresome in this time of climate change, but when in doubt, make

Sometimes a good microclimate is simply that spot in your yard where there is not only plenty of sun but a fence or other structure to offer shelter from wind and help keep the area a touch warmer.

conservative choices—choose, say, a cultivar rated to zone 5 when you garden in zone 6.

Mesoclimate

A site's mesoclimate depends on the mitigating effects of topography, such as proximity to a mountain or a large body of water. For example, the south side of Lake Erie has particular climatic characteristics that set it apart from other areas nearby: the moderating effect of the lake makes it possible to grow certain raspberries and other fruits that could not otherwise survive at this northern latitude.

Another example of a mesoclimate is the north slope of a mountain, which experiences colder absolute temperatures and less warming temperatures early in the season as compared to a southern exposure. This difference might determine whether or not certain cultivars or even species could reliably be grown. Again, when in doubt, hedge your bets and

choose plants that are considered comfortably within your zone, not borderline.

Microclimate

Microclimate is the last and smallest of the three locations. Technically, the term is used to describe very local conditions, such as the temperature or relative humidity within a canopy of a plant, but it is often used more broadly to describe the conditions at an individual site—your own yard. In most of North America, weather is monitored from a range of locations, and the USDA and some universities supply the information to the public. Researchers are even looking into using GPS (Global Positioning System) to pinpoint weather conditions down to a square foot. Such data are useful for making a first cut at characterizing the climate of your garden, but honestly, the best knowledge is that gained by careful observation of a plot of soil over time. Nothing beats determining the conditions of the specific site for yourself.

Maximum/minimum thermometers, which have two columns of mercury to show the lowest and highest (as well as current) temperatures, are inexpensive and readily available at most garden centers and farm supply stores. Rain gauges are another useful and easy-to-find tool for assessing your property's particular conditions. You may be surprised to find differences between your observations and those made on a site only a few miles away.

A common home-scale microclimate is a slope. For many berry plants, a higher spot in the yard is better than a lower spot. Cold air rolls downhill, so when you are planning to grow something that likes warmth, plant near the top, not at the bottom; there is less chance of frost damage in an elevated spot, not to mention better air flow and better drainage.

Growing conditions on a sunny slope up against your house's foundation may differ dramatically from those in a hollow at the far end of your property. Another microclimate factor is moisture, which often concentrates in lower-lying areas of your property, even if the spot doesn't show water pooling right on the surface. Some berries like damp ground (blueberries, for example); others will struggle or perish. Be observant, and be practical. It's always easier to match a site to a plant than to labor to modify a site.

SOIL FERTILITY

In our increasingly nonagrarian society, soil is right up there with our most underappreciated resources. It took millions of years for soil to form and build up the rich reservoir of nutrients so essential to the growth of our plants—yet a significant amount of it can be washed away in a single downpour. Treat your soil as the precious commodity that it is. It is correctly called "dirt" only if you find it on your kitchen floor.

When thinking about soil fertility, remember that berries are perennials. The expected life spans of these plants range from a few years (strawberries) to decades (blueberries). The level of nutrients and organic matter in the soil before you plant is critical—think of it as preventive nutrition.

If you suspect your yard's native soil is low in fertility, you can and should improve it, not just for your incoming berry crop but for practically anything else you might want to grow. To add nutrient amendments to the soil, use a spade or rototiller to mix in any of the relatively immobile nutrients (phosphorus, lime, sulfur) as much as possible. The more water-soluble nutrients (nitrogen, potassium) should be worked into the top 6 to 12 inches (15 to 30 cm) of soil for best results. Nitrogen can also be top-dressed later in the season, and/or in subsequent growing seasons, if your crop requires it.

Organic matter is key

Organic matter in the soil (by way of materials such as chopped-leaf compost, rotted sawdust, decomposed manure, and spent mushroom compost) is the Holy Grail of gardeners for several reasons. As organic matter in the soil breaks down, a reservoir of nutrients is slowly released and made available to plants. Organic matter also improves a soil's ability to attract and hold onto nutrients, preventing them from washing through to the groundwater. This is especially beneficial for berry plants.

When organic matter is added to soil, the clay aggregates are broken apart, creating an environment that is more hospitable to plant roots. Organic content also contributes to a soil's tilth or friability—that is, how easily the soil breaks up into smaller pieces. Soils with a lot of heavy clay tend to form clumps in your hands and do not break up into smaller pieces easily. Again, most berry plants do best in high-quality, readily workable soil that is high in organic matter.

Soil tests

While you might not be inclined to run a soil test for just any new plant, it's a good idea to do so when getting ready to grow berry plants. It's not just a matter of liking fertile ground that is well drained: several berry plants also prefer more acidic conditions.

You may find you need to make some adjustments.

Ideally, a soil test should be conducted in August or September, prior to the spring when you intend to plant. Many Cooperative Extension offices across the United States offer soil tests or can refer you to a private laboratory; in Canada, there are provincial and private laboratories. Yes, you will have to pay for the test, but it won't be much, and it is worth it for the valuable information and the peace of mind.

Follow the instructions supplied to you on how to collect the sample(s). Be sure to tell them that you plan to grow berries, and what kind; appropriate plant recommendations will be returned to you, depending on your soil's pH and nutrient profile. Results typically come back with suggested amendments for your garden soil as well. Follow these! But note: a regular soil test is not exhaustive or comprehensive. The elements that are not checked (nitrogen; micronutrients) are nonetheless important.

Soil pH

This is a measure of the concentration of hydrogen ions, which is a reflection of how acidic or alkaline the soil is. Old-timers used to refer to this as the "sourness" or "sweetness" of the soil, because they would literally taste the soil to make an assessment (luckily, the invention of the pH meter eliminated the need for this down-and-dirty method). A pH of 7.0 is neutral: anything higher indicates alkalinity; anything lower indicates acidity.

Most garden plants, including many berries, thrive in soils with a pH of between 5.5 and 6.5. Such a pH level is optimal because it provides an environment in which nutrients can be readily taken up by the plant. However, some berry plants—including blueberries, cranberries, and lingonberries—like soil that is more acidic. So, again, make sure the lab knows what plants you're thinking of growing so they can make appropriate recommendations.

If your soil is not quite in the right range, you can nudge it. If it is too alkaline, sulfur may be recommended. On the chance that your soil is actually too acidic, you'll be advised to incorporate lime. Such amendments take time to move through soil, so if required, you should add them as soon as possible—ideally, in the fall before you intend to plant.

Soil nutrients

There are different ways to supply amendments, and every gardener has their favorites. Be comfortable with your choices, using what is available in your area and within your budget. Good organic or natural sources are legion—see the suggestions with each element here, bearing in mind that nutrient analysis for each of these materials is bound to vary somewhat. Overall, please remember that good, decomposed compost is often sufficient for supplying most of what most berry plants like—in other words, in most cases you can't go wrong adding compost to a site.

You can use inorganic or chemical fertilizers, if you prefer. If you do, be careful to not only acquire the right material but to diligently follow the product's application directions in all matters, including timing; refer to your soil test results for amounts.

Phosphorus is responsible for energy transfer in the plant and is important for the production of flowers, fruit, seeds, and roots. It is found in numerous enzymes and required for protein synthesis. Common symptoms of phosphorus deficiency are a general stunting and a darkening and/or reddening of older leaves, as well as poor flower and fruit formation. Because phosphorus, like lime and sulfur, is not very water-soluble, it moves slowly in the soil and should therefore be added the fall before planting. Organic sources include bonemeal, rock phosphate, fish bone meal, soy husks, colloidal calcium phosphate, most composts.

Potassium is involved in many biochemical reactions in plants. It ensures general vigor and increases a plant's resistance to drought and disease. Deficiency often results in small

When a raspberry plant is growing in soil that is magnesium-deficient, the leaves become yellowed and puckered.

root systems. Potassium is intermediate in water solubility, so it can be added in the fall or the spring before planting. Organic sources include greensand, sheep manure, dried seaweed or kelpmeal, granite meal, wood ash.

Magnesium is a nutrient that is needed in smaller quantities than potassium. It is often found lacking in small-fruit crops, so soil test results regarding this nutrient are particularly valuable. Deficiency symptoms include the yellowing (chlorosis) of older leaves. Like potassium, it is intermediate in mobility in the soil and can be applied in fall or spring. Organic sources include crushed eggshells, Epsom salts (magnesium sulfate), bonemeal.

Nitrogen is the most crucial element for garden plants. It is the basic element in proteins, which are fundamental components of plants and animals, and is also an essential element in chlorophyll, which gives plants their green color—hence, inadequate nitrogen will result in pale green leaves. To generalize, nitrogen enhances the growth of leaves and stems—plants really need it, and berry plants are no exception.

Because it is very soluble in water, nitrogen moves readily in the soil. It should be applied just before or after planting, or each spring when the plants resume growth. The recommended amount of nitrogen can also be apportioned into several smaller applications throughout the growing season to provide a continuous supply. This method may be particularly useful if your soil is sandy (nitrogen leaches through sandy soils readily). Organic sources include most any composted animal manure, alfalfa meal, soybean meal, bloodmeal, fish emulsion or fish meal, worm castings, used coffee grounds, grass clippings.

Micronutrients

Micronutrients (iron, copper, zinc, and others) are elements that plants need in minute quantities (measured in parts per million). Most micronutrient deficiencies occur when the soil pH is not in range.

Why have lawn when you can grow edible plants? This gardener recognized that a sheltered, sunny backyard had the potential to become a lot more interesting, not to mention productive.

Soil tests rarely include a micronutrient analysis because micronutrients are much more accurately measured from the leaves of the plants, rather than from the soil. Unless you know in advance that your soil lacks a particular one, you will not correct for micronutrient deficiencies before planting. If you suspect a deficiency in an established plant, you can probably order information, via leaf or tissue analysis, from the same place that performed your soil test. The good news is that most soils have sufficient micronutrients, and a significant deficiency in home gardens is unusual. Organic sources include kelp meal and granite meal.

Cover crops for soil fertility

After you've staked out an area for your new berry crop and removed the weeds, grass, or other plants that were growing there, you now have open ground. If you've dug in compost and other nutritious amendments in readiness for your hungry plants, you certainly don't want the spot invaded—or recolonized—by weeds, or all that good stuff carried away over the winter months. A cover crop is a good solution. It will hold the spot, preventing erosion; winter rains or snow won't carry the soil away; and the cover plants should crowd out encroaching weeds, too. As it gets closer to berry-planting time, you can plow the cover crop under. When returned to the soil next spring, the cover crop will contribute organic matter as well as some nutrients.

What sort of cover crop depends not only on what you can get at your local garden center but when you plant. Winter rye, for instance, can be sown later in the fall because it is able to germinate in colder soil. Alfalfa, clover, or vetch can be sown in the spring or summer months.

If you've never done this before and it sounds like a good idea to you, track down

Among the things that can block needed light are buildings, fences, and trees. Since most yards are not entirely free of such obstructions, the best you can do is observe and site your berry plants in a spot that receives maximum light.

good advice specific to your area and give it a try. Just remember—dig in the cover crop next spring at least three weeks prior to putting in your berry plants. The plant debris needs time to break down in the soil, and while doing so, it can tie up nitrogen.

TOO MUCH OF A GOOD THING?

Too much direct, hot sun can be a problem. If you are raising certain berries, such as raspberries, in a hot climate, you'll want to protect your crop from UV damage. Creating a tunnel over the planting will do the trick and has the added advantage of shielding the plants from heavy summer rainshowers, which can damage them.

MORE SITE CONSIDERATIONS

You want to think about a variety of things before you even break ground or go shopping for your berry plants. Consider and make decisions about the following matters.

Light requirements

"Can I grow berries in shade?" This is the question most frequently posed by aspiring berry gardeners. The short answer? Not if you want fruit, and probably not if you want healthy foliage, either. For most all types of berries, more sun equals more fruit.

What qualifies as full sun? Six hours of direct sunlight per day, at a minimum. Granted, to find a backyard site that is not shaded by any obstructions can sometimes be a challenge because both landscaping and houses (yours and neighboring ones) may

Ground that drains poorly, such as soils with high clay content or ones that are compacted, is not a good place to grow most berries. The roots will struggle for oxygen and may rot, and plants will suffer.

The same sort of raised bed in which you might raise vegetables, herbs, or flowers is just fine for strawberries. A bottomless wooden box 8 to 10 inches deep (20 to 25 cm), filled with organically rich soil, will provide these shallow-rooted plants a good home.

dramatically reduce available light. Be flexible—possibly the sunniest spot may be in your front or side yard, rather than out back.

Also know that a few shade-tolerant exceptions do exist. Gooseberries and currants will usually survive and produce some fruit when planted in areas with filtered shade. Blueberries also tolerate shade quite well, but they usually produce few flowers and fruit under these conditions; they make wonderful ornamentals, however, turning lovely shades of red and yellow in the fall.

Drainage

Making sure that your soil drains sharply is another essential aspect of site selection. If an area puddles and holds water for more than a few hours after a rainstorm, it probably is not suited to growing berries. If you are not certain whether your soil is well drained, get out the shovel. Dig a hole 12 to 24 inches (30 to 60 cm) deep and look for any yellow or gray mottling in the soil. If you see such mottling anywhere less than 18 inches (45 cm) deep, the site is probably marginal. If possible, leave the hole open and observe how quickly water drains after a rainstorm. If water sits there for more than 12 hours, the site is not appropriate for berry plants. Fortunately, many such sites can be improved by digging in organic matter prior to planting. Heavy clay soil with poor drainage, however, is often beyond hope and help.

Berries in raised beds

If you conclude that your soil is just not suitable—the quality is too poor or the ground drains too poorly—you can always bring in good soil for your plot. Strawberries will grow well in simple mounded beds, around

A deep raised bed or large containers make raising blueberries possible, if your soil is poor or not acidic enough. This tack alleviates other issues, too: tending won't involve as much bending over, any tunneling rodents can be thwarted, drainage will be good, and harvesting will be easy. To hold the root systems of these shrubs, this sort of raised bed ought to be 15 to 20 inches (40 to 50 cm) deep; pots ought to be 7 gallons or larger.

12-1 DRY
PINTS

You might begin your berry research in earnest by visiting a nearby pick-your-own farm. Many of these have a range of cultivars within each berry time, and you can taste-test and bring some home to consider. Somebody there will be able to tell you the names of the ones you and your family like best. A local berry farmer is also a good person to ask about which selections do best in your particular area.

10 inches (25 cm) above grade, something you can accomplish by hand if you have to. For the rest of the berries, raised beds are a possible solution.

Raised beds for berry production are likely to be different from the ones in which you would raise favorite vegetables. They ought to be deeper, generally speaking—12 inches (30 cm) is good, 15 to 20 inches (40 to 50 cm) is even better. Fill with good, organically rich soil, amended with plenty of compost. Berry plants love it.

If you would like to grow raspberries and blackberries in raised beds, make the beds longer and/or wider, as these brambles tend to become big, sprawling plants. Also, it's wise to attach any supports to the beds themselves prior to putting in the plants.

CHOOSING YOUR BERRIES

What berries do you like? It would be silly to grow plants that do not make your eyes sparkle and your mouth water at their very mention. Start with what you like and then narrow it down by considering what can be grown easily on your site.

You may also want to consider whether

you want to grow berries that require processing. Few of us have a palate for raw black currants, but this fruit makes wonderful juice. Elderberries, likewise, are not for the timid if fresh consumption is the goal, but they work beautifully for pies and jams.

Selecting cultivars

For each berry crop treated in this book, cultivars are suggested for different regions, according to the recommendations of experts in those areas. These regional divisions are based on similarities in climatic and soil conditions.

The regions cover broad geographical areas and thus should be used as guidelines rather than absolutes. If, for example, you live and garden in southern Quebec, you will want to select the hardiest of the selections recommended for the Northeast. In the Midwest, a Minnesotan might opt for the half-high blueberries developed for that region, whereas a grower in Georgia would go for rabbiteye or southern highbush blueberries. In California, most raspberries are best adapted to the cool, coastal climates of the Pacific Northwest, but certain varieties will also tolerate the hot southern and central valleys. As always, consult local sources such as Cooperative Extension personnel and other gardeners. Their experience is invaluable.

Another consideration is your own yard's conditions. If you haven't got much space, make plans for smaller or fewer plants and/or seek out cultivars that are more compact. If you have ample space, and your climate permits, however, consider extending your harvest season by putting in varieties that ripen at different times (early, midseason, late)—as many as you can fit and care for!

Buying plants

The best strategy is to buy directly from a reputable nursery. All plant labels should

NOT A BERRY NICE GIFT

Unlike accepting seeds, accepting the gift of berry plants from another gardener can be a bad idea. Their plants may harbor diseases or other pests that are hard to discern with the naked eye. Gauge the level of vigor and productivity of the planting in its current environment, then carefully examine the plants offered for disease symptoms. Even well-intentioned, kind people can give away viral Typhoid Marys, so if you elect to obtain plants from someone else's garden, be aware that you are taking a risk that may develop into a liability.

provide the species or cultivar name and indicate that the plants are virus-tested and certified. Avoid purchasing from nurseries where the plants are not clearly identified; nursery catalogs that carry berries and other small fruit only as a sideline should also be avoided.

It's also a good idea to patronize a nursery in your part of the world, although this is not a hard-and-fast rule. Sometimes a gardener in Oregon may wish to order that special gooseberry from Indiana. Just clear your choice with the nursery beforehand—if you are ordering by mail, send them an email or give them a call first (there may be other restrictions; a few places still ban some or all gooseberry and currant cultivars; check with your supplier). A list of retail nurseries that specialize in and/or offer an ample selection of berry plants can be found at the back of this book.

Whatever you do, wherever you get your plants, remember to make a note of the names of the cultivars you have acquired. This can be useful if you run into any problems, or if you later decide you want to replace them, get more, or try different ones.

POTENTIAL PROBLEMS

Generally speaking, berry plants are not especially sickly or troublesome. Nonetheless, forewarned is forearmed when it comes to pests. Pests are any living organisms that injure your plants or harvest—not just insects and other creepy-crawlies but diseases, weeds, and vertebrates (birds, deer, berry-swiping kids—probably not the early morning joggers, though you never know!) as well. Diseases are probably the most common threat; weeds too must be kept at bay. Specific pest problems are described in the subsequent chapters on individual berry crops; discussed here are some general concepts and philosophical issues.

Remember, a happy, healthy plant is a pest-resistant plant. Those that are struggling due to poor location, excessive shade, excessive cold, drought, overwatering, nutrient deficiencies, or neglect are much more likely to become afflicted. Establish a healthy planting, maintain it well, and you won't see many problems.

Diseases

Diseases in plants, like those in humans, are caused by microorganisms. But plants, unlike mammals, do not have immune systems. Most plant diseases are caused by viruses or fungi, though a few bacterial diseases also affect plants.

Berry viruses will drain and in some cases ultimately kill a berry planting. Learn which viruses might damage your crops. Not all are immediately fatal or cause for panic. For instance, while some strawberry cultivars will succumb to virus pressure in a year or two, others will tolerate viruses quite nicely for many years. The reality is that all berry crops have viruses associated with them, and the impact ranges from not-even-noticeable to the death of the plants. Become familiar with what associated damage looks like. Learn how to prevent or mitigate viruses. Don't plant near wild berry patches. And buying certified virus-free stock in the first place is key, of course.

Fungal diseases are usually instigated by spores that are ubiquitous in the atmosphere. Once these spores come into contact with a plant—under the right environmental conditions—they grow and develop on it. In the case of a pathogen (a disease-causing agent), this is always to the detriment of the plant. As with insect pests, some diseases (such as gray mold, caused by *Botrytis cinerea*) affect the fruit directly; others grow on foliage or invade the root system.

In general, wet conditions exacerbate disease problems. Extended periods of rainy weather, over-irrigation, or conditions that

When weeds get into your berry patch, there's trouble. Weeds will greedily consume soil nutrients and moisture that your plants need, not to mention create crowding problems. Intervene early and often so this doesn't happen!

hamper the drying of dew, such as shade in the morning hours, can all increase the likelihood of disease. Careful cultural management of your prized berry plants, such as pruning and thinning overly dense foliage and eliminating weed populations, can reduce the threat of disease.

Weeds

Weeds are simply plants that are out of place, at least from a gardener's perspective. When they are growing next to your berry plants, they are directly competing with them for the precious resources of light, water, nutrients, and space. Reducing these resources will limit the growth and productivity of your crop plant—not good.

Weeds also limit air circulation around the plants, which prevents moisture from dew or rain from drying off as quickly. Many fungal diseases that infect berry plants thrive in wet environments, so a crowd of weeds can tip the balance in favor of disease. Weeds can also harbor insects or, worse, viruses that can infect and harm your fruit plants. Dandelions, for example, are widely infected with tobacco ringspot virus. If a nematode takes a bite out of an infected dandelion and then feeds on your raspberry roots, the raspberries will become infected with the virus,

If you cover your berries to keep out pests, just make sure sun, air, and water can still reach them.

producing a symptom called crumbly berry that ruins fruit quality. The only cure at this point is to remove the raspberry plants—hardly an appealing "control."

Prevent weeds at the outset by doing an excellent job of site preparation. If the area is overgrown, and/or if there are perennial weeds present, being thorough now will save you a lot of heartache later. Solarize, mulch, or—if you're willing and have weighed the risks and benefits—carefully apply a weed-killer, such as a systemic herbicide containing glyphosate.

After your plants are installed, prevent a comeback by yanking, hoeing, or mowing weeds out if you spot a resurgence—early intervention is best and easiest, of course! Do not use weedkillers (herbicides) at this time; they could potentially harm your berry plants. You can lay down a layer of mulch.

If you do a good job of weed control in your crop's first season especially, it gives the plants a fighting chance. In subsequent years, as your plants fill in and grow more robustly, they should naturally shade out and crowd out any encroaching weeds. Weeds tend not to grow well in a healthy, well-filled-out canopy of berry plants.

Insects, mites, and slugs

Only a small percentage of the hundreds of thousands of insect species in nature are pests, but those few can cause a lot of damage. Some injure the fruit directly by feeding or laying eggs on them. Others damage the plant by sucking sugars from the leaves or by consuming the leaves and roots, thus indirectly affecting fruit yield. Some insect pests also transmit viruses, which tend to debilitate the plant over time.

And it's not just insects. Slugs can exact a disheartening toll on a strawberry planting, particularly in wet years. And mites—tiny insect-like creatures more closely related to spiders—are often found on the undersides of leaves; remedies that control insects often have no effect on mites, and vice versa.

Acquiring and maintaining healthy plants is your best weapon against such pests. But should any appear, act early and prudently. First make sure you know what pest you're dealing with—leaf damage, for instance, can be due to any number of things, and you shouldn't leap to conclusions. Consider the symptoms and signs described in this book, and confirm your suspicions with a local expert or via Cornell University's online diagnostic tool (see "Further Reading and Resources") if you can. Only then can you plan appropriate action.

Neighbors and other vertebrates

Vertebrates are animals with backbones— deer, raccoons, voles, mice, rabbits, birds, and so forth. They can cause problems with and even considerable injury to small-fruit plantings. Deer feed directly on leaves and shoots; they especially relish raspberries. In times of desperation, however, they will feed on almost anything a gardener plants. Mice and rabbits can nibble away the base of fruit plants. Sometimes mice or rabbit populations become so dense that they damage a plant's root systems with their burrowing. And—last but not least—hungry birds will raid a berry planting, stripping away the fruit just as you are ready to harvest.

A few words on human pests: ripe, home-grown berries are pretty irresistible, and some people just can't resist. The neighborhood kids taking a few berries is probably no big deal (there's plenty to go around), but if you go away for a weekend and come home to find a bush stripped, it might not be birds or critters—the culprits might be human. You can put up "Do not touch," "Please ask first," or even "Pick your own, $3 a pint" signs, along with an "honor box" and some baskets or bags. If you ever catch the raiders, perhaps you could suggest they pick your ripe fruit for you, and earn a share of the harvest in payment!

CONTROLLING PESTS NATURALLY

Each grower of berries has to determine how aggressive he or she wants to be in managing pest populations. The extent to which you need to control pests in your planting also depends on how much you can tolerate losses of fruit and plants. For example, commercial growers would want to control tarnished plant bug (*Lygus* spp.) because their customers don't want deformed fruit, but a small infestation would be much less of a problem for a home gardener because, honestly, the slightly deformed berries taste just as good. Being armed with a few facts will help you decide.

There are many good reasons to water your berry plantings at ground level. Chief among them? There is less waste, and both berries and leaves stay dry, which helps prevent rot diseases.

Pests that cause direct damage to your berries, such as slugs or sap beetles, pose a more immediate threat than indirect pests such as aphids or mites. Many of these pests can be controlled with cultural (pesticide-free) methods. Once you start seeing excessive injury to your plants, however, such as leaf discoloration from mites, leaf deformation by aphids, or leaf destruction by Japanese beetles, it's probably time to get more actively involved.

Just as each of us arrives at a personal or spiritual philosophy in our own way and in our own time, the same is true for developing our gardening or pest-management philosophy. Obtain information, make informed decisions, and follow your gut feelings. One strong piece of advice for all gardeners, however, is that approaching your garden or pest issues blindly and without careful thought will be neither satisfying nor successful. Substitute knowledge for rote application of chemical pesticides, and you have the basis for integrated pest management.

Many of the best pest-management techniques, including with respect to raising berry crops, require no chemicals at all. Establishing a healthy plant stand in an appropriate site with an optimal density, and maintaining it in good health, goes a long way toward preventing and controlling problems. Here's a summation of safe, spray-free, organic strategies.

Choose a good site. The importance of appropriate site selection bears repeating. The conditions of a site will have a profound effect on pest problems throughout the life of a planting. Well-drained soil will eliminate most root rots; exposure to sunlight will speed the drying time of the leaves, thus reducing fungal leaf and fruit rots.

Solarize the soil. This method uses high temperatures produced by capturing radiant energy from the sun to, literally, fry soil-borne pests, such as weeds, fungi, bacteria, and nematodes and other insects. It's an easy and inexpensive way for you to improve the soil and reduce the likelihood of pest problems.

Cover the soil with a clear plastic tarp for approximately four to six weeks; black plastic doesn't work as well because it doesn't let light in. The plastic sheet will trap the sun's energy in the soil and heat the top 12 to 18 inches (30 to 45 cm), thus killing a variety of soil-borne pests. This method works best in warmer climates, such as the South and West, and is effective only when the weather is hot, such as at the height of summer and works less well at other times. Also, if you till up the area a bit and dampen it and/or add some fresh poultry manure, soil solarization is more effective. Yes, some minute, beneficial soil organisms may be impacted, but research has shown that they tend to recover and return.

Choose resistant cultivars. Finding out which cultivars recommended in your area are resistant to pests or diseases is an important step. Certain strawberry cultivars offer excellent resistance to root rots, and others have some resistance to fruit and leaf fungal diseases. Some raspberries are resistant to the raspberry aphid, a pest that transmits debilitating viruses. Not only is resistance a factor, but cultivars that are well adapted to your area will grow better and will resist disease and insect infestation by virtue of their good health.

Water the roots, not the plants. Damp plants and especially damp fruit are more vulnerable to problems, especially diseases that lead to rot. And yet, you need to keep your plants evenly moist, especially at that critical period when berries are forming and ripening. So, don't use sprinklers! Use trickle irrigation from a soaker hose or emitters, or

A tidy berry patch, generously mulched, is a healthy and happy berry patch. Not only does mulch help keep weeds at bay, it conserves soil moisture so you don't have to water as often.

even go to the trouble and expense of installing an in-ground irrigation system. Whatever you decide, the object is to apply small but steady amounts of water to the soil at the base of your plants.

Keep plants free from weeds. Weeds not only weaken a berry planting by competing for water, nutrients, and sunlight, but they can slow the drying of moisture within the plant canopy, thus encouraging the proliferation of fungal diseases. Prevent weeds with a good mulch, and pull any that sneak in.

Maintain appropriate plant density. Keeping rows well spaced, shoots thinned out, and vines well trained fosters good air circulation around your plants. This not only allows them to dry more quickly following a rain or watering but can also prevent fungal spores from settling or germinating on the leaves. Maintaining a good plant density is done by renovation in strawberries, maintaining narrow rows in suckering raspberries and blackberries, and by pruning in all other berry crops.

Harvest ripe fruit and get decaying fruit out quickly. If ripe berries are not going to be consumed right away, pick them as they ripen on the plants and store them away in a freezer container. You can process the frozen fruit later, when the garden is not demanding so much immediate attention.

When fruit rots do appear, be sure to remove the rotted fruit from the planting. Although pulling a rotten raspberry or strawberry off a plant is not pleasant (sometimes you have to sort of squish them off), leaving it on the plant creates a source of infection for every nearby ripening berry.

THE LAST RESORT

Chemicals in the berry patch? If you're like most home gardeners these days, you don't like to spray, certainly not your edible plants. Let commercial growers do this if they must; one reason you are growing your own berries is so you have control over how they are managed.

However, there might come a day when you reluctantly consider spraying. For certain insects and diseases, and in certain years, certain products may be your only option. Or you might have inherited or rehabilitated an older planting, and you're unwilling to surrender and watch it decline, suffer, and die. Just be sure that you know what you are doing and why you are doing it.

If the plants are really in bad shape, you might be wiser to tear them out, destroy or dispose of the remnants, and start over another day. But should you decide that a chemical battle is worthwhile, proceed with great caution. Remember, whether naturally occurring or synthesized by humans, herbicides and pesticides are by definition toxic. Some guidelines and tips:

- Correctly identify the problem or culprit.
- Check with a local expert (Cooperative Extension agent, master gardener, or even a local contractor with a pesticide-application license) to identify the right product for your problem. Herbicides kill unwanted plants, fungicides kill fungi, insecticides kill insects, and miticides kill mites.
- Use only products that are labeled for the plant to which they are being applied.
- Always follow the directions on the label to the letter. Do not apply more than the recommended dosage indicated on the label, but do not apply less either. Too-low dosages can encourage the gradual buildup of resistance in a population of pests.
- Do not use the same product continually. Although many newer pesticides are formulated to reduce the ability of pests to build up resistance, rotating for a given pest is advisable.
- Never apply insecticides during bloom time, since it will kill the bees that pollinate the flowers. Applying pesticides in the evening will also limit bees' exposure to them.
- Evaluate the treatment's effectiveness. If it's not satisfactory, stop, and revert to complete removal—and destruction—of the afflicted plants.

IT IS HARD TO IMAGINE AN ENTITY WITH

more aesthetic appeal than a berry, each with its own vibrant color, sensual shape, often inviting smoothness, and fruity fragrance. The fact that this perfect package of utility and form is borne on plants which themselves offer such variety of shape, form, and color only adds to its allure.

A currant bush studded with ripe berries is a striking sight in a garden. Most ornamental gardeners focus on what flowers can bring to a scene, forgetting too often that berries also contribute color and beauty.

Why, then, aren't berry plants used more frequently in the landscape? There are two answers to the question. One is that many gardeners are simply not familiar with berry-producing plants. The second is that, in addition to their fabulous possibilities, certain berry plants have signature pitfalls. Rather than seeing these as immutable shortcomings, though, we can develop more realistic expectations about how the plants will perform by better understanding their limitations.

Taking our cue from the familiar vegetable bed, we usually plant our berries in rows—but this is more often out of tradition or habit than necessity. Every chapter in this book includes specific suggestions for using each berry in more creative ways. Before jumping into the discussion of your preferred plant, however, take the time to look over the general concepts presented here for working berry plants into the landscape.

Small-fruit plants can take a variety of forms, from low groundcovers to rounded

BERRY PLANT FORMS FOR THE LANDSCAPE.

1. low groundcover: strawberry
2. upright groundcover: lowbush blueberry, lingonberry, cranberry
3. rounded shrub: gooseberry, currant
4. low clustered canes: half-high blueberry
5. medium clustered canes: highbush blueberry
6. tall clustered canes: elderberry, Juneberry

shrubs to long-trailing vines, and they therefore have a similar range of landscape uses. Familiarizing yourself with a plant's expected form and ornamental characteristics is an important first step in planning your edible-yet-attractive yard. Some specific suggestions for using berry plants follow, but feel free to use your imagination. Your garden space is unique, as are your tastes, needs, and environment, and the best way to use the plants in the landscape is however they best suit your situation.

GROUNDCOVERS AND EDGINGS

Strawberries, lowbush blueberries, lingonberries, and cranberries make terrific groundcovers or small edging plants. For neutral soils (pH 5.5 to 7.0), low-growing strawberries are an especially good choice: you have only to plant a few and they will quickly fill in the space with runners and daughter plants. You could also use non-running alpine strawberry (*Fragaria vesca*) as an edging around beds (bearing in mind that you will end up replacing them after a while). Nothing

Lingonberries, planted closely and allowed to spread out a bit, make a truly handsome groundcover or edging plant.

Even a densely planted garden could accommodate a strawberry plant or two.

is lovelier than a healthy strawberry canopy in bloom with flowers that are large and white with bright yellow anthers. The yielding of early spring flowers to fruit is a wonderful process to observe, particularly to those of us starved for plants after a long, dreary winter.

Perfect for more acidic soils (pH 4.0 to 5.0), lowbush blueberries (*Vaccinium angustifolium*) form a carpet of delicate flowers followed by deep blue berries and, later in the season, fiery fall foliage. Lingonberries (*V. vitis-idaea*)—which at 12 to 18 inches (30 to 45 cm) high are slightly more upright than most groundcovers—have an equally striking presence in the landscape with evergreen foliage and dazzling red berries.

Well before any berries appear, a berry plant can still contribute interest. Here a small blueberry bush studded with flowers fits right into a mixed bed.

If you're already growing other edibles such as vegetables and herbs, why not incorporate some berries?

Strawberry plants are pretty even before the berries appear. The perky white flowers hold up well and can be sited so they will stand out in your garden.

Brambles—that is, raspberries, blackberries, and their kin—can be grown as a hedge or property-line "living fence." Be sure to install supports earlier rather than later and make sure they are strong enough, as mature plants are full and heavy.

One way to help these ground-floor berry plants shine in your garden is to position them for contrast. White pebbles or light-colored gravel in a walkway, the backdrop of gray or buff rock walls or fencing, or redwood bark mulch are all materials that naturally highlight encroaching or draped berry plants. In other words, don't let them get lost to the eye next to green lawn grass.

HEDGES AND FENCES

What better way to seclude yourself from a busy world than with a fruitful plant as a hedge or fence? Besides obvious privacy benefits—blocking an unpleasant view, keeping pedestrians or pets out of your yard,

mitigating street noise—hedges can also act as barriers or be used to define or clarify boundaries, such as a property line or entryway.

The potential berry plants to use in this

CREATIVE SUPPORT

While it is true that the healthiest, most productive raspberries and blackberries need appropriate support—full details are in their chapter—it could be fun to sacrifice a little productivity for style. A bramble could be persuaded to adorn a decommissioned orchard ladder, a large old wagon wheel, or a discarded wrought-iron gate. Browse an antiques barn or estate sales for inspiration.

The red stems of blueberry bushes—which you may not notice in the summer months—stand out well in the winter garden, adding a touch of beauty to your yard during an otherwise quiet time of year.

way are numerous. Elderberries (*Sambucus* spp.) can be used to construct a thornless hedge up to 12 feet (4 m) tall. The form of the flower cluster is reminiscent of an umbrella, the ensuing clusters of dark purple fruit have great visual appeal, and thanks to a stream of introductions from plant breeders, the leaf colors and forms of elderberry are more diverse and exotic-looking than ever. In more acidic soils, try a blueberry hedge. The blueberry bears exquisite little bell-shaped flowers in clusters. In autumn, leaves of most cultivars turn a vibrant red or yellow, a refreshing alternative to the overused burning bush (*Euonymus alatus*). Once the leaves fall off, the plants reveal red stems that rival the popular red-twigged dogwoods in intensity and hue. Not to mention that the fruit is wonderful, too.

Blueberries lack thorns and do not produce suckers to irritate (or enthrall) your neighbors. Sometimes, though, thorns can be a good thing, if, for example, you want to present a formidable barrier to someone or something. In this case the gooseberry could be your plant of choice. Gooseberry plants

If you value your privacy and good autumn color equally, consider planting a hedge of well-mannered blueberries. Imagine—you get this glorious fall show *and* tasty berries in season!

As long as you have a sunny spot for them and are good about watering, there is no reason why you cannot enjoy a bounty of berry plants in pots on a patio or deck.

make a terrific thorny hedge, 3 to 6 feet (1 to 1.8 m) high, which tolerates more shade than the average fruit plant. The leaves of many gooseberry cultivars turn a striking red in the fall, and the shapes and colors of the fruit also provide interest.

Berries can also be trained to grow on existing fences. Thornless blackberries will drape over a sturdy one, though they need to be tied on at intervals since they lack tendrils.

CONTAINER DISPLAYS

Many of the berry plants in this book can be successfully grown in containers rather than planted directly in the ground. You may choose to grow berries in containers out of necessity (limited or nonexistent yard space). Or perhaps you want to keep the plants out of reach of slugs or within better reach of you and your family (no stooping or stretching).

You might also do this simply because a container planting is a valuable design

You might also enjoy growing and displaying strawberry plants in a hanging basket. Just remember to water consistently, to keep them looking good and to help them produce a good crop.

A mix-and-match border like this makes it easy to look after all your berry plants and follow their ripening processes; it's a one-stop area of the yard you'll enjoy monitoring consistently.

element on its own. Imagine two large ceramic pots filled with blueberry plants flanking your doorway—a beautiful feature which just so happens to provide easy access to berries for breakfast picking. Strawberry pots are a favorite on a sunny patio or deck. Classic terra-cotta is always nice, but a pot with a cobalt blue exterior glaze would make a stunning picture when the red berries dangle down the side. Long planter boxes, along a porch or deck, are another option. Another fun idea might be to tuck plants into an old orchard bin or fruit crate.

Some creative gardeners have managed to incorporate containers of berry plants to interesting effect. Picture an old wine barrel with a half-high blueberry placed at the intersection of paths in a formal herb garden, or urns of luxurious strawberries in the company of other red flowers in adjacent pots—geraniums, begonias, even a fiery crocosmia or canna. A gooseberry in a tub, espaliered against a courtyard wall, is an automatic conversation piece. A crate of cranberries shoulder-to-shoulder with a vegetable garden is an inviting, intriguing sight.

As berry production progresses and then begins to slow, a patch can start to look more raggedy. This is par for the course; plan for it, and you won't be troubled by this phase.

A HANDFUL OF PITFALLS

"Uh-oh," you say. "Pitfalls!?" Unfortunately, it's true. Though it's easy to wax poetic about a berry plant's wonderful combination of usefulness and beauty, we are all best served by being fully informed about possible difficulties before we sally forth to create our edible landscape. Perhaps this section is more appropriately called "considerations" rather than pitfalls. At any rate, do consider the following points before you plant. Not only will you have realistic expectations, but you will be more careful about siting berries in appropriate locations around your home.

Crop maintenance is not optional. While ripe and healthy fruit is lovely to look at, rotting fruit on ill-cared-for plants is truly unattractive. This unattractiveness goes beyond the visual, as rotting fruit can take on unpleasant smells and attract unwelcome insect visitors. Also, many berry plants require pruning during their dormant period, and failing to carry out this essential task is inviting disaster. Pruning not only ensures a crop of good-sized sweet fruit, it keeps rows

There are times when berry plants simply don't look neat and tidy, which, while a small price to pay for benefitting from their tasty harvest, is something to consider when siting them in your home landscape. You want to plant them where their less-pretty times and their informal or bulky profiles are not an issue.

of plants neat and narrow and the leaf canopy open, so light and air can penetrate.

The "unattractive" stage. Most perennial landscape plants go through "unattractive" stages—periods when they are not at their most ornamental. Strawberries are a good example. They make a lovely lush groundcover in the fall and spring, but after fruiting in early summer they go through a quasi-dormancy, during which time they look, for lack of a better word, ratty. At this point you need to renovate the strawberry patch, removing leaves and thinning out the plants (full details are in their chapter). They regrow by about midsummer, so the plants are at less than their best for only a short time. Still, keep this aspect in mind as you plan your planting. And before deciding what to do about your plants in their "off" seasons, you should carefully read the sections in this book dealing with the specific berries.

The "not there at all" stage. Apparent disappearance is another common trait in garden perennials, including your potential berry plants, and being aware of it is vital to proper siting. Fall-bearing raspberries, for example, are often cut down to the base during the dormant season. As a result, the plants will seem to be gone entirely—not good for a hedge or fence! One idea is to plant your fall-bearing raspberries against a foundation, with spring-flowering bulbs and perennials in front. With this arrangement, first the bulbs and then the low-growing perennials flower and take the stage; as all this is happening, the green stems of the raspberries provide a lovely backdrop at an important time.

Some berries are thugs. Suckering, erect blackberries and raspberries leap to mind, but even the humble strawberry can be invasive in the right environment. One way to control the growth of the plants is to "containerize" them in the soil. You can place barriers, such as substantial pieces of plastic made for this purpose, along the edge of where you want the plants to grow and stay. Sink them securely into the earth—you're trying to hold back questing roots.

The issue of invasiveness brings up another potentially sensitive issue: neighborly relations. Though red raspberries make a wonderful hedge (and the summer-bearing types are present all year round), if you plant on or near a property line, suckers will come up in your neighbor's yard as well as in your own. One option is to install barriers to minimize these unwanted suckers, and hope all goes well. Alternatively, talk with the neighbor. Some will embrace the idea of a raspberry hedge if you offer to let them harvest the fruit from their side!

strawberries

STRAWBERRIES—SUCH SMALL PLANTS,

such beautiful fruit, such wonderful flavor! But the quality of store-bought strawberries is generally unimpressive—too often these luscious fruits are produced far from where they are consumed. Strawberries grown in places like California and Florida, which have longer growing seasons than most and depend on shipping the bulk of their harvests out of state, are not picked for optimal flavor. Oh, they are good cultivars, valued for yield, color, and firmness. But the demands of the produce and shipping industries mean that they tend to be harvested too early, while still green. They do color up in transit but, alas, their flavor does not correspondingly improve. Also, these strawberries tend to be heavily sprayed, further impetus for you to raise your own.

One of the many joys of growing strawberries is that the plants are so attractive in season—even before the berries appear, you can enjoy the foliage and flowers.

The good news is that you can easily grow strawberries in your own yard, and the flavor can be fantastic. Think of the strawberry as the tomato of the berry world: the difference between those that you can buy in the grocery store and the ones you grow in your own backyard is like night and day.

From a purely ornamental point of view, strawberry plants make lovely low-growing groundcovers or edgings. Their glossy, medium dark green leaves are handsome through early summer and turn red in the fall. Strawberries are also productive—they grow quickly and lushly.

Strawberries have been around, and appreciated, for a very long time. The first written reference is from ancient Rome, but the berries were likely collected from the wild for medicinal purposes and as a source of food well before recorded history.

The Chilean strawberry (*Fragaria chiloensis*) had been cultivated extensively in Chile for at least two millennia when, in the early 1700s, it first made its way to European gardens; there it was cross-pollinated with the North American native *F. virginiana*. The hybridization of these two species led to the development of today's commercial strawberry, *F.* ×*ananassa*. The hybrid was clearly superior to all other strawberry species

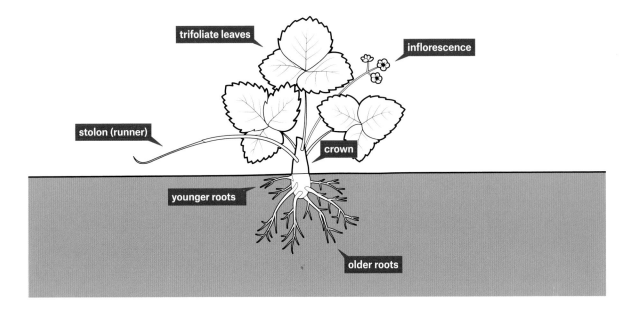

trifoliate leaves

inflorescence

stolon (runner)

crown

younger roots

older roots

available in Europe at the time, and since then, breeding efforts continue to improve fruit quality, productivity, pest resistance, cold hardiness, and various ornamental qualities.

Traditional plantings of the Chilean strawberry began to wane in the 1950s, when they were mixed with northern hemisphere cultivars of *Fragaria* ×*ananassa*; they have been largely replaced by California-bred cultivars. Several expeditions to Chile by North American researchers have sought to collect and preserve some of these remarkable Chilean strawberries—they are valuable for their genes alone.

Today, strawberries are produced in every U.S. state and in nearly every country in the world, most notably Italy, Poland, Russia, and Japan. This wide distribution suggests that the strawberry plant is widely adapted, and as a genus, this is true. However, many individual genotypes or cultivars of strawberries are narrowly adapted to local conditions, and so selecting cultivars that are proven to perform well in your specific region is key.

ABOUT THE PLANT

The strawberry plant is in many ways unique among fruit plants. It is an herbaceous perennial composed of leaves, a crown (a compressed, modified stem), and a root system. The root system has two types of roots: those that are semi-permanent, lasting for more than a season, and those that are transient, lasting only days or weeks. In light sandy soils, the roots may extend as deep as 12 inches (30 cm), with half of the root mass in the lower 6 inches (15 cm). In heavier soils, such as clay loams, 90 percent of the roots may be located in the top 6 inches (15 cm) of soil. This explains, in part, the plant's sensitivity to water—or the lack of it—in the soil.

Another aspect of the strawberry plant that has practical importance to gardeners is that new roots arise from the base of the developing leaves. Since leaves (and along with them, roots) are formed successively higher on the crown as the plant ages, the strawberry tends to grow "out of the ground" or rear up. For this reason, you should mound soil around the base of the plants at renovation time (see "Renovation of June-bearers" on page 76 for details), particularly as the bed ages. This practice supports the base of the plant and gives the newly forming roots a place to call home.

The runners or stolons (which form the daughter plants) arise from buds in the leaf axils and are the strawberry plant's means of asexual propagation. Runners form during the long days of summer; they generally require a daylength of more than 12 hours for formation. The matted-row system of growing—information on that is ahead—takes advantage of the plant's runnering capacity as a means of establishing many plants from a few.

The flower cluster (technically, the inflorescence) of the strawberry plant arises from the terminal buds. Bud formation occurs deep in the plant tissue and is invisible to even the most observant gardener.

The inflorescence formed from this single bud contains a number of flowers, which will result in a number of fruits. Expect about 30 days between flower opening and fruit ripening. The terminal, or king, flower opens first. It will yield the largest fruit, appropriately called the king fruit. Unfortunately, since it opens first, the king flower is also more likely to be damaged by late frosts.

The remaining flowers on the inflorescence open sequentially down the truss, from top to bottom. In other words, the second flowers to open are those located just below the terminal flower. They will open slightly later (usually a day or two) and have slightly smaller fruit. Thus the fruit is smaller as the season progresses.

If branch crowns (small compressed branches on the thicker main crown) have

On any given strawberry plant, the first flower to bloom becomes the first flower to develop into a fruit. This king flower, as it is known, will also yield the biggest fruit on the plant.

developed, more than one inflorescence may be borne on a single plant because each branch crown can terminate in a flower cluster. After several years, however, if too many branch crowns develop on an individual plant, intra-plant competition for resources can result in smaller (albeit more numerous) berries. So, three- to four-year-old plants are not as desirable in a planting bed as younger plants, which have fewer crowns. (For more on longevity, see the sidebar on page 75.)

The strawberry itself is an aggregate fruit, composed of achenes (a type of seed) that are fused together on a tissue (the receptacle) at the end of the flowering axis. The majority of the consumable portion of the fruit, therefore, is technically receptacle tissue. Fruit size, which ranges from ¼ inch (0.5 cm) to 2 inches (5 cm), is dependent on a number of factors, including the fruit's location on the inflorescence, the density of the crowns on an individual plant, and the particular cultivar. Certain cultivars are simply larger or have less variation in size within a given cluster.

As for what the harvest looks like, environmental factors certainly play a role. How much water the plants receive and how dense the planting is can affect fruit quantity and quality. Color varies among strawberry cultivars from fairly light orange to very dark red or near purple—bright red may be the familiar norm, but it does not always happen and does not always indicate ripeness. Suffice to say that you'll have to get to know the ones you decide to grow.

Most important of all, know that strawberries—unlike some other fruit crops—are self-fertile. This means that only one cultivar is required for fruit production. Thus growing different cultivars or types may be done simply because you want to try different ones; they should all produce, and they won't need to cross-pollinate.

STRAWBERRY TYPES CHEAT SHEET

June-bearing (short-day). The most popular. You get one big crop in June or so (earlier in warmer climates). Produce lots of runners.

Day-neutral. Best in cooler areas. These deliver a steady supply of berries throughout the summer months under moderate temperatures and, often, into the fall. Produce some runners.

Everbearing. A bit of a misnomer, these older cultivars give one big crop in early summer and another, smaller round in fall. Produce few runners.

Alpine. Small berries, big taste, from a different species altogether. Plants generate berries on and off all summer. Can be grown from seed. Produce no runners.

STRAWBERRY TYPES

The different strawberry types are defined primarily by their time of flower bud initiation, and hence, time of fruiting. The two main types are June-bearing (short-day) strawberries, which initiate flower buds when the days are short, and day-neutral strawberries, which will form flower buds regardless of daylength unless the temperatures are too warm. Strawberry types can also be distinguished by the different species from which they were bred. Again, most cultivated strawberries are hybrids, *Fragaria ×ananassa*. The alpine strawberry (*F. vesca*) is not as familiar but is easy to grow and delicious.

June-bearing (short-day) strawberries

The short-day strawberry is by far the most widely grown, widely available type. It bears its fruit over several weeks in May and June in most regions of the northern hemisphere; it grows well in zones (4)5 to 10. Flower buds form during the short days of autumn (late September through early November), become dormant in the winter, and then flower and fruit when the weather turns warm again in spring. These plants generate a lot of runners, which in turn develop leaves, flowers, and fruits of their own.

Temperatures below 60°F (16°C) are ideal for bud formation; generally, night temperatures over 70°F (21°C) are not good for the plants. Some bud formation might continue through the short, warm days in spring as well. A plant needs a full, well-established leaf canopy because the leaves provide the energy for flower bud initiation. It's also important to note that the daylength response relates only to when flower buds are formed; it has nothing to do with when the plant actually blooms.

Day-neutral strawberries

Day-neutral strawberry plants are able to produce flowers and fruit throughout the growing season (as long as temperatures stay below about 90°F, 32°C). This takes a lot of energy, so the berries are generally not as large as those of the June-bearers, though they are still of good quality.

Day-neutrals initiate flower buds regardless of daylength, thus producing some fruit almost continuously from spring through fall. (The catch is that they are at their best in cooler summers—very hot summers or cycles of hot spells make set and output unpredictable.) They will flower and produce fruit and runners simultaneously. Also, runner plants often flower prior to rooting.

In their first year in your garden, you'll get a fall crop. By their second year, day-neutrals start fruiting at roughly the same time as the June-bearing strawberries, usually between mid-May and mid-June. At this time, plants produce a medium-sized crop of medium-sized fruit. In the middle of the summer, expect another small crop, plus a few scattered berries in between. The midsummer crop is often the smallest in

Alpine strawberries are smaller than regular strawberries. Their fruit shape tends to be more elongated as well. Flavor is amazing!

size, particularly in warmer climates, and may suffer from the heat, drought, or insects prevalent at that time of year. Plants resume fruiting in earnest again in late summer (August in most cases) and will continue until the first hard frost.

Speaking of a good fall crop, you can use a trick the commercial growers use, if you want. Plant every spring. Rely on the newbies to provide your fall crop that first year. Meanwhile, tear out your two-year-old plants after harvesting their spring crop.

Day-neutrals are great for gardeners with limited space. They are easier to control in raised beds, planter boxes, and containers than other types. Runner production isn't heavy and you can easily remove unwanted ones. Indeed, you can enjoy a good harvest with only, say, a dozen or so plants.

Because they have relatively low root-to-shoot ratios, these are especially sensitive to high soil temperatures. Help them out and cool the soil with a heavy straw mulch or white plastic. In general, day-neutrals are a better choice for gardeners in cooler climates, that is, zone 6 and colder. In warmer areas, try planting them in the fall and start harvesting the following spring.

Everbearing strawberries

Everbearing strawberries, which generate a good crop in early summer and another, smaller one in fall, should not be confused with day-neutral strawberries. They initiate most of their flower buds during long days and tend to lack the productivity and berry quality of the day-neutrals. They don't generate many runners, compared to the other types, which makes them suitable for anyone

TYPICAL STRAWBERRY HARVEST TIMES

	June-bearing strawberries	Day-neutral strawberries
California	January–May	April–November
Northeast	mid-June–mid-July	mid-August–frost*
Southeast	February–April**	December–March**
Midwest	mid-June–mid-July	mid-August–frost*
Rocky Mountain	mid-June–mid-July	mid-August–frost*
Northwest	mid-June–mid-July	mid-August–frost*
Southwest	March–June**	December–October**

* And again the following June, if you hold them over. ** Longer along the coast.

with less garden space to devote to strawberries. Depending on the cultivar and where you garden, you can have success with these anywhere from zone 3 to 9.

Everbearing cultivars are occasionally offered in retail nursery catalogs. Overall, the day-neutrals have eclipsed them in popularity due to better fruit quality and higher yields.

Alpine strawberries

These are a different species, with much tinier but intensely sweet strawberries. If you've never seen or heard of them, it's because alpine strawberries are not grown commericially; they are too little and fragile for grocery stores or even farmers' markets. But you can grow them at home—and they can be wonderful.

Though it is less well known than the June-bearing strawberry in North America, the alpine strawberry (*Fragaria vesca*) is actually the most widely distributed type of strawberry plant, occurring throughout Europe, northern Asia, and North America. Also referred to as *fraise des bois* or wood strawberry, these are especially popular in France, where they are considered a real delicacy (specialty farmers provide them to boutique restaurants).

These small herbaceous perennial plants can be used as ornamentals as well as for fruit production—that is, they are attractive and tasty. Unlike regular strawberries, they don't form runners. Instead, over time, the plants become ever-larger, soft mounds, individual plants topping out at 10 to 12 inches (25 to 30 cm) high and wide. Thus, they're great in pots, baskets, and windowboxes. Able to tolerate light shade, they generally perform better in cooler areas. For instance, alpine strawberries can grow along a woodland path, provided they get sufficient water and occasional fertilizer.

These are day-neutral, so they generate fruit continuously from spring through fall. Smaller plants than the hybrid strawberry of commerce, alpines produce correspondingly tiny (½ inch, 1 cm, or less), cone-shaped fruit that—when ripe—is aromatic and utterly delicious. Each one is an explosion of sweetness, with hints of pineapple. A few on your cereal or yogurt can be just the thing in the morning!

Alpine strawberries do have a vulnerability, in some areas. They can be susceptible to viruses, which shorten their life span. If this happens to yours, you may be tempted simply to replace them and carry on.

They're not always easy to find in North America. Scan the offerings of nurseries that

'Cavendish'

specialize in fruit. Or order seed—unlike their hybrid cousins, they are easily raised from seed. Hardy in zones (3)4 to 9.

CHOOSING THE RIGHT CULTIVAR

To succeed in growing healthy strawberry plants that yield a delicious harvest, choose your type and cultivar carefully. Strawberries are extremely sensitive to local conditions, and a cultivar that performs well in one location may do poorly in another, so start local:

- If you know another gardener in your neighborhood or town who is growing strawberries, ask them what they advise. (But turn down gift plants and don't replant runners. Always start fresh with robust, healthy young plants.)
- Check with local master gardeners or your nearest Cooperative Extension Service office to see which cultivars they recommend.
- Ask at your local farmers' market, farmstand, or pick-your-own farm; your favorite berry vendor could be a great source of advice and information.
- If you just want to test the waters, so to speak, create a small plot and see how it

goes for a season or two before committing to digging up, preparing, and planting a larger area.

To extend or stagger your harvest, use the same trick you may already be using in your vegetable garden—grow a few different cultivars. The typical June-bearing strawberry bears ripe fruit for only about two weeks, but by including early, midseason, and late cultivars in a planting, you can enjoy ripe strawberries from the backyard for as long as six weeks during late spring and early summer.

Alternatively, extend your season by growing different types. Plant some June-bearers as well as some day-neutrals. But be careful: June-bearers produce runners, while day-neutrals produce few, and you don't want the June-bearers to crowd out the others. If you try this, give them separate areas in your yard, or at least sufficient space in separate rows.

Use the recommendations in the cultivar lists as guidelines only: your particular growing region or microclimates in your own yard may allow you to explore beyond those listed. Except for the alpine strawberries (*Fragaria vesca*), all are selections of *F. ×ananassa*, the hybrid garden strawberry.

'Honeoye'

'Hood'

June-bearing strawberries

'Allstar' NE MW Midseason. Produces flavorful, elongated berries that are lighter in color than those of most cultivars. Good fruit size. Productive. The standard midseason berry in the Northeast and Midwest.

'Annapolis' NE MW Early. Fruit medium in size, moderately firm, and glossy, with good flavor. Plants runner freely.

'Benton' NW Mid to late season. Fruit moderately soft; bright red with excellent flavor. Plants are vigorous, high-yielding, and runner well.

'Camarosa' SW Early to midseason. Fruit is larger and firmer than otherwise similar 'Chandler'. Brilliant red color.

'Cavendish' NE Midseason. Large, firm fruit with good flavor. Productive and moderately vigorous. Tends to ripen unevenly in hot years.

'Chandler' SE SW Early to midseason. A productive plant with large, flavorful berries. Tender.

'Earliglow' NE MW Early. Small, soft berry with excellent flavor. Plant is only moderately productive. The standard for early cultivars.

'Honeoye' NE MW RM NW Midseason in the Midwest; very early in the Pacific Northwest. Large fruit, productive. Fruit tends to become soft in hot weather. Flavor is distinctive, perfumey; can be bitter in some locations.

'Hood' NW Early to midseason. Fruit large, bright red, and quite firm. Classic strawberry flavor. Outstanding processed as frozen fruit; one of the main cultivars used in ice cream making! Plants are not long-lived.

'Jewel' NE MW RM Midseason. Large, soft fruit; can be very dark. Tends to soften in hot weather. Very productive, dense foliage.

'Kent' NE MW Midseason. Extremely productive plant with large, firm fruit. Yields fruit in middle of the plants, resulting in high incidence of rot, so planting rows should be kept narrow. Average flavor.

'Puget Reliance' NW Midseason. Big yields! Soft, juicy, slightly acid flavor that is perfect for jams and jellies. Large red fruit.

'Totem'

'Seascape'

Erect growth habit, which helps hold berries off the ground a bit, thus preventing rot.

'Sequoia' SE RM SW Early. Produces large, dark red berries with excellent flavor. Thrives in dry, hot climates, provided it gets adequate irrigation.

'Shuksan' NW Early to midseason. Large, unevenly shaped, glossy fruit with moderately firm flesh and good flavor. Lots of runners; a big plant over time.

'Sparkle' NE MW Late. Flavorful, high-quality, attractive but soft fruit. Plant tends to grow very thickly. Size decreases rapidly during harvest season. Tolerates heavier soil than other cultivars.

'Strawberry Festival' SE SW Early to midseason. A newer variety that produces lots of runners. Conical fruits are on nice long stems (pedicels); they are firm, flavorful, and bright, glossy red.

'Sweet Charlie' SE Early. High productivity and good fruit quality. In Florida, the standard against which all other cultivars are compared.

'Sweet Sunrise' NW Early. Large firm fruit with excellent flavor. Excellent red color throughout the berry. Open plant makes fruit easy to pick. Vigorous. Outstanding processed as frozen fruit.

'Tillamook' NW Midseason. Vigorous. Very large, firm fruit with excellent red color throughout; fruit must be left to ripen fully or it will be bland. Open plant makes fruit easy to pick. Outstanding processed as frozen fruit. Standard in the Pacific Northwest.

'Totem' NW Midseason. Large, dark red fruit with red interior color. Good processed as frozen fruit.

Day-neutral strawberries

'Albion' NE SE MW RM NW SW Long, conical, bright red berries with excellent flavor. Justly popular and widely grown.

'Monterey' NW SW An outstanding new selection, developed in California. Larger fruit than 'Albion' but not as firm. Excellent disease resistance but susceptible to powdery mildew in some areas.

PRETTY IN PINK

Have you ever seen the pink-flowered strawberry? 'Pink Panda' was developed in England as an ornamental—for groundcover use, to trail over a rock wall, or to sprawl in a hanging basket or other ample container. The pink color came about by crossing marsh cinquefoil (*Comarum palustre*) and cultivated strawberries. It grows about 12 inches (30 cm) high and, with runners, has a spread of up to twice that. The perky pink blossoms begin in spring and continue into summer. Unfortunately, the foliage sometimes obscures them. Also, berries may be sparse and, though sweet enough, birds may beat you to them. Overall, you'll want to grow this one for its beauty.

There are a few successors: 'Ruby Red' ('Franor') has redder flowers, those of 'Gerald Straley' are scarlet, and newer 'Lipstick', with deep pink flowers, produces larger, more flavorful berries.

'**Portola**' **NW SW** Another newer California cultivar. Similar in size to 'Albion', but it ripens earlier and the color is lighter. Excellent flavor.

'**San Andreas**' **NW SW** This newer California cultivar was derived from 'Albion'. Fruit color is lighter, flavor is exceptional. Fewer runners than other day-neutrals.

'**Seascape**' **NE SE MW RM NW SW** Large, firm fruit with good flavor. It doesn't require much chill so can be planted in warmer climates. Very productive.

'**Tribute**' **NE RM NW** Berries are medium-sized, slightly larger (and later) than 'Tristar'. Flavor not as strong, and plants are more vigorous.

'**Tristar**' **NE NW MW RM** Fruit is smaller than that of 'Tribute' and size is further reduced in hot weather; a trick to increase berry size is to grow where there is morning shade to delay ripening a bit. Flavor is wonderful. Firm flesh and skin. Moderate vigor. Bears an early crop.

Everbearing strawberries

'**Fort Laramie**' **RM** Produces medium-sized, very soft, aromatic, bright red berries that are particularly suitable for freezing and preserving. Hardy.

'**Ogallala**' **MW RM** Small, dark red berries with sweet flavor. Fair yields compared to others. Good drought resistance. Excellent cold hardiness.

'**Ozark Beauty**' **NE MW** Medium-sized, uniform, wedge-shaped red berries. High yields. An old-timer, very popular—considered by many to be the best everbearer.

'**Quinault**' **NW** Medium-sized and brightly colored, inside and out. Fruit is delicious but tends to be a bit soft, so must be harvested and handled with care. Able to produce berries on unrooted runners.

Alpine strawberries
All may be grown in most of North America, that is, in zones (3)4 to 9.

'**Alexandria**' Mounding, compact plants produce a steady supply of ruby-colored fruit. Tasty, fragrant berries are larger than many of the other alpine cultivars. This is the most commonly available selection.

'**Mignonette**' A dainty-looking French heirloom cultivar, grows easily from seed. The small, pointed, red berries have a delicate hint of almond flavor.

'Rugen Improved' A German cultivar. The scarlet fruits are larger than other alpine cultivars. Sturdy plants form small mounds.

'Yellow Wonder' The "white alpine" cultivar. A productive plant with fragrant, delicious, pale yellow berries; it may take some trial and error to discover when it is at peak ripeness and best flavor. Easily grown from seed.

SITING AND PLANTING

Begin your strawberry adventure by giving your new plants the best possible chance of success: select a really good spot and get it ready ahead of time.

The right spot

Ideally, you should select the site of your strawberry bed the year before planting. This allows proper soil preparation (testing and amending), an essential first step toward a successful harvest. Strawberries should not be planted where potatoes, tomatoes, eggplants, peppers, or black raspberries have had a problem with verticillium wilt, as strawberries are also susceptible. Many cultivars are resistant to the pathogen that causes this fungal disease, but none are immune.

Also, if you can, avoid a site that was formerly lawn. The grubs that infest grass sod roots consume strawberry roots as well.

Plus, grass can become a persistent weed presence in the planting. If you have no choice, there are ways to minimize potential problems. Break up the sod, then dig the soil as deeply as possible, keeping an eye out for grubs. If you see them, expose them to the air and/or remove them by hand. Repeat this process until you no longer see any of the pests. Solarization of the soil will also decrease the grub population. Be sure to take care of this problem prior to planting.

Sites that are heavily infested with weeds like sedges (*Carex* spp.), nutgrass (*Cyperus rotundus*), quackgrass (*Elymus repens*), Johnson grass (*Sorghum halepense*), bindweed (*Convolvulus* spp.), or Canada thistle (*Cirsium arvense*) should also be avoided.

Light and soil requirements

Strawberries require a lot of sunshine to succeed and produce a good crop—at least 8 to 10 hours of direct light every day. If you have a choice, plant your strawberries where they will get their sun in the morning (eastern or southern exposure), so that the dew will dry quickly, reducing the chance of fruit rots.

Strawberries also need adequate air drainage. A gentle slope lessens the danger of spring frost damage to flower buds by improving air flow, although steep slopes (that is, over 12 percent) should be avoided because it's harder to tend your plants and the soil can erode.

Strawberries are best planted in loose, workable ground. Handle the roots very gently, and do not bury a plant's crown.

Strawberry plants can grow in many soils, from sand to heavy loam. Best yields, though, are obtained in deep, fertile soils that have good internal drainage and high levels of organic matter. It's good practice to improve the site in any case by digging in well-rotted manure or other organic matter.

Nor are strawberries especially sensitive to soil pH, though they grow best in the 6.0 to 6.5 range. Soil should be tested the spring or summer prior to planting. This way, you can dig in any recommended additives in the fall prior to planting. (Note that phosphorus is key for healthy root growth and good fruit production in strawberries—refer back to "Soil Nutrients" on page 18 for sources.)

Because of their shallow root systems, strawberry plants are particularly sensitive to water in the root zone, either too much or too little. Soils that have poor drainage induce smaller root systems (due to reduced oxygen for root respiration). Poor drainage also encourages fungal diseases that may infect the roots. If it would be a lot of work (or near impossible) to bring a site up to snuff, you can raise strawberries in raised beds filled with organically rich, well-drained earth.

Buying plants

Get dormant strawberries from a reputable nursery in the spring—they are generally sold in bundles as bare-root plants. Make note of the seller's claims about plant health (for example, virus-indexed or virus-tested) as well as their guarantees. Inspect the plants to make sure there are no insect pests and that they are in good condition. Once you get them home, trim off brown or damaged topgrowth or straggly roots. Discard moldy ones. If you can't plant right away, store the plants in a shady area or a refrigerator.

Plant them as soon as the soil can be worked. Planting once summer is underway (June to July) is not recommended—it's too late and it's too hot.

Young plants will look very small and insignificant at first—but take heart. They will grow and flourish, given time and tending.

Once the baby plants are safely in the ground at evenly spaced intervals, water them well.

Planting day

Early spring is the ideal time to plant straw-berries in most areas. Do not try to plant them in semi-frozen or soggy soil; wait until the ground thaws out and dries a bit. Fall planting is better in mild-climate areas (Southern California, areas of Florida and the Gulf Coast).

If possible, pick a cool, overcast or drizzly day to minimize stress on the baby plants. About a half-hour prior to planting, soak the roots in water. Then, be careful that roots do not dry out during the planting process. Lay a damp cloth over them and take plants out one at a time.

Dig a hole as deep as the roots on the transplants, about 6 to 8 inches (15 to 20 cm) deep for each, and set in place without cramming or bending the root system (if necessary, trim it to fit). Do not bury the crown; cover the plant with soil to just below it. Then water well so the roots get a good soaking. Afterward, lay down a good mulch—see "Caring for Your Plants," later in this chapter, for full details.

Planting plans

Fans of homegrown strawberries as well as those who grow them professionally for farmstands or market have developed various ways of setting them in the ground. Some methods take up more space and/or

June-bearers, or short-day types, produce lots of runners, which in turn produce daughter plants. Planting them in rows works best.

require more effort than others. Also, some work better for certain types, so review the following information with care. Consider also whether harvest quantity or quality is your priority.

No matter which layout or style you end up choosing, actual planting of individual plants is the same.

Matted rows. The primary method for raising June-bearing strawberries is the matted-row system. In the initial planting, mother plants are spaced widely. The subsequent daughter plants fill in the gaps to create a dense block of plants. The strawberry's perennial nature is used to best advantage

in the matted rows by allowing the plants to be replenished with new growth each year. If properly maintained, a matted-row system can yield strawberries for many years.

Plant your June-bearers 18 to 24 inches (45 to 60 cm) apart in rows 3 to 4 feet (1 to 1.2 m) apart, with the soil line above the roots but not covering the growing point of the crown. The wide spacing of the plants makes for a relatively inexpensive initial investment, and the plant's ability to form runners freely allows it to create a dense bed in the first season. Lay down mulch to keep opportunistic weeds out while you wait for the bed to fill in. Runners will spread out

VARIATIONS ON THE MATTED-ROW SYSTEM

Ribbon rows. This style requires more plants, but you'll get fruit the first year, which is appealing. Space plants closely, about 4 inches (10 cm) apart, in rows 3 feet (1 m) apart. Clip off runners as they appear, but leave flowers to develop into berries. This concentrates the plants' energy. The drawbacks? It's labor-intensive, and productivity declines after about three seasons. But it could be worth a try!

Staggered rows. This method is best for day-neutral and everbearing strawberries. Set plants close together, about 5 inches (13 cm) or more apart. Array them in staggered double rows if you like that look. Note that day-neutral plants are sensitive to warm soil temperatures, so they should be mulched immediately after planting with about 4 inches (10 cm) of clean straw.

VARIATIONS ON THE HILLING SYSTEM

If growing strawberries this way works well for you, there are a couple of modifications you can try in subsequent years. All runner plants in these two variations should be set about 5 inches (13 cm) or more apart.

Single hedgerow. In this system, allow each plant to produce and root just two runners.

Double hedgerow. This variation allows several runners per plant, so perhaps provide a little extra elbowroom between the mother plants when you first set them out.

and root. You'll get lots of berries with this scheme, though the size might not be as good as the hilling system, described next.

Hilling system. The other main way to grow strawberries is the hilling or mounding system; if done correctly, you'll get good crops of larger berries. This method is best for cultivars that do not runner much, especially the everbearing and day-neutral types. It allows easy access for clipping out any and all runners, as the mother plant is the one you want producing berries. Deliberately concentrating the plants' energy in this fashion causes more flower stalks, and thus more fruit, to form. Some plants also respond to having their runners removed by generating extra crowns next to the main crown; these too flower and fruit.

Here's what to do: position plants 12 to 15 inches (30 to 40 cm) apart in rows. Separate rows by several feet so you'll be able to patrol them with your clippers.

This system makes for a highly productive bed. So productive, in fact, that your plants may run out of steam after the first season—making them, essentially, annuals that you have to replace every year.

In mild climates, you can plant in the fall and anticipate a spring harvest. In colder areas, plant in spring and harvest in summer and fall.

Raised beds. It's easy and practical to raise strawberries in raised beds. They get the room they need to roam, and the entire project is neatly self-contained. Just be sure to pick a spot that is sunny all day long

Many gardeners prefer to grow strawberries in a raised bed, not only because it elevates the crop for easier access to the berries, but because it makes it so easy to provide the good soil and good drainage plants need to prosper.

Strawberries are easy to grow in raised beds. If you site the bed in a sunny spot and fill it with fertile, well-drained soil, plants will thrive. Note that this gardener set up the raised beds on a cleared-off surface, which not only keeps encroaching lawn and weeds at bay but helps make working in and around the beds more comfortable.

and near a water source; close to the house is good, too, if you can manage it. Raised beds are also a good idea in areas where the native soil is lousy.

As for dimensions, you can experiment, but a "box" 8 inches (20 cm) deep and 3 feet (1 m) wide works well. This way, the roots have ample space and water can drain away. And the narrow width allows you to reach in easily to care for and harvest your crop. Line the bottom with screen if digging rodents are an issue, and porous landscape fabric if you need to separate your good soil mix from any contaminants that may be lurking below. Frame it with rot-resistant wood such as cedar (avoid chemically treated lumber), stones, bricks, or plastic.

The mix for raising strawberries should be fertile and well drained; one-third rotted compost or other enriching organic matter combined with two-thirds clean topsoil is good. As for spacing the different types of strawberries in a raised bed:

- June-bearing cultivars: plant 12 to 18 inches (30 to 45 cm) apart; this allows space for their runners.
- Day-neutral, everbearers, and alpines: plant closer, 8 to 12 inches (20 to 30 cm) apart.

Strawberries in containers

If your space is limited, if the soil in your yard is unsuited to strawberry cultivation, if hungry slugs are a big problem, or if you just have a good sunny spot for pots—grow your strawberries in containers. It's such a joy to behold hearty plants, studded with bright red, tasty berries, right on your porch, deck, or out your back door!

Among your choices are pyramid planters, hanging baskets, strawberry pots, and grow bags. Pyramid planters, which hold soil in rings or squares with successively smaller rings or squares stacked on top of the base, are available from many garden supply stores and online sources. Strawberry pots are vertical urns that come equipped with multiple "pockets"; glazed ceramic pots are more pleasing to the eye than the plastic kind and less likely to dry out than unglazed clay (terra-cotta). Hanging plastic grow bags (which you can drape over balcony or porch railings) and narrow planter boxes (which attach to the top of the railings) are perfect solutions for growing strawberries in tight quarters.

Keep in mind that fruiting may not be as prolific as plants grown with more traditional methods. Choose your containers carefully, however, and the aesthetic bonus will make up for any loss in productivity. A few tips for success:

Strawberry pots, which are readily available from any garden supply store, are a fun and easy way to grow the berries.

There's no rule that says you can't grow one strawberry plant per small pot. In fact, a cluster of these in the corner of a deck or patio can be a charming sight.

- Fill the container of your choice with well-drained potting mix. (If it's a big container, no need to fill the entire thing with soil; strawberries are shallow-rooted. Set in stones or like material in the bottom and ladle the mix on top.)
- When inserting each little strawberry plant, gently wrap each root bundle in a small piece of damp newspaper, so you can tuck it into place without mess or harm (don't worry: the newspaper breaks down shortly thereafter).
- Water often! Pots in sunny spots dry out fast.
- Mulch the surface, if you can, to prevent the medium from drying out.

- Site the container where it will get ample sun and be out of the wind, and where it's convenient for you to monitor it and to pick berries as they ripen.
- If getting enough water, evenly, to the roots becomes an issue, try one of the following: mix water-absorbing crystals into the soil mix; insert a perforated pipe down the middle of the pot; place a perforated plastic jug on top and let the water leak in slowly.
- Feed your container-grown strawberries monthly during the growing season with a balanced fertilizer, diluted at half-strength. (This is more than you would feed in-ground plants.)

Here's a variation on the strawberry pot. You can buy one of these or fashion your own, and enjoy both the look and the modest harvest wherever space is short—on a patio, deck, or balcony. Just make sure drainage holes are part of the package, as roots can rot in a soggy mix.

CARING FOR YOUR PLANTS

Mulching

Strawberries appreciate mulch. Immediately after planting them, apply a good mulch to help conserve soil moisture and keep weeds at bay. Position it around the plants and in the rows between them, but don't push it up onto the crowns of the plants, which might encourage rot. Don't use decayed or wet leaves, which tend to mat down and can smother the baby plants. Many growers favor straw (not hay—hay contains seeds).

If you garden in an area with cold or freezing winters, you should mulch again and with a heavier hand in the fall. See "Overwintering," page 77.

Watering

A newly installed strawberry bed should be watered immediately after planting. Then, the plants should receive at least an inch (2.5 cm) of water per week, either from rain or supplemental watering. Be especially vigilant about this requirement in the very first year so the plants can become well established.

Even after your plants settle in, it's important to pay close attention to

One key to healthy, productive strawberry plants is a good thick mulch around the plants and between rows.

watering your strawberries because, being shallow-rooted, they are particularly vulnerable to drought. Watering plants in the morning so that the foliage has time to dry before nightfall is best—it helps prevent leaf diseases.

Depending on the size of your patch and the dryness of your climate, there are various ways to deliver the necessary water. Hand-watering or overhead sprinklers may be fine. But you will waste less water with soaker hoses or a trickle or drip irrigation system—these might be worth considering.

Soaker hoses are easy to use. Lay these directly on the soil in your strawberry bed, either to the side of the rows or between rows. Trickle or drip watering involves a system of small emitters that slowly release water directly into plant root zones. Some are above-ground, attached to a garden hose; others are sophisticated rigs that are installed below the soil before planting (best, of course, in climates where the soil never freezes, as you'll leave them in place).

In any event, targeted, timely watering is the key to a good and tasty harvest. Wait till the strawberries appear and begin to enlarge, then ramp up your attention to watering—check the plants every day, if necessary. There is usually a learning curve, however; you need to strike a balance. Too much water at this critical time and the flavor

STRAWBERRY FIELDS FOREVER?

If you live in an area where winter cold does not harm or kill your strawberry plants, you may get several years out of an individual plant before its output slows. Of course, diseases and other pests (discussed later in this chapter) can also affect a plant's durability and shorten its life span.

The productive period, and longevity, of a strawberry patch varies. Much depends on your climate and the plants you have chosen. With good care, including removing and replacing aging ones, some beds keep going for many years. That said, many gardeners choose to treat their day-neutrals and everbearers as annual crops.

If you're a diligent steward of your June-bearers—promptly renovating every year after harvest, as described on page 76—they'll reward your efforts. Yet some who raise these hedge their bets and plant a second patch in a different part of their yard, so that while one is producing, the other is ramping up to replace it the following year.

Neglected strawberry beds of any sort are a sad sight. They soon become jammed with competing plants, including opportunistic weeds. Berry production, of course, declines. Older plants eventually start pushing their crowns up and out of the ground, which leads to winter damage. If you are guilty of neglect or if you inherit an unloved patch, your best bet is to rip out everything, improve the soil, and start over with new baby plants.

---

of your berries will be diluted, even bland. Erring on the dry side will result in smaller fruit, but more intense flavor.

Fertilizing

Organically rich soil—which you made sure of before planting, yes?—ought to yield satisfactory crops and delicious flavor. Market gardeners and commercial strawberry farmers need to fertilize strawberries, and you might consider providing extra nutrition if you decide your plants could use a boost. Fertilizer goes alongside the plants, or mixed into the soil if mounded; always water it in well so it can reach the roots and get taken up by the plants.

Feed your June-bearing strawberries twice: right after planting and again in late summer. The standard dose is 2 pounds (1 kg) of a 10-percent nitrogen fertilizer per 100 feet (30 m) in each row. Organic gardeners can use an organic, water-soluble plant food, such as seaweed, fish emulsion, or a blend.

Day-neutral cultivars require a more constant nitrogen rate throughout the planting year. You may apply 1 pound (0.5 kg) of ammonium nitrate per 100 feet (30 m) of row once a month in June, July, and August. Organic gardeners can use bloodmeal, mixed into the soil surrounding the plants; the recommended rate is a half-pound (0.25 kg) per 100 square feet (30 m²).

In subsequent seasons, you'll have to judge whether your plants need to be fed. If the soil seems to become depleted or the plants are increasingly less robust or vigorous, by all means do. (Or consider whether to divide the plants, or to start a new, improved bed elsewhere and give this area a rest—read on for more information about these tacks.)

Pinching

Little or no strawberries to eat the first season? You may be reluctant, but there's good reason to pinch and be patient. It avoids stress on your baby plants, letting them devote energy to developing roots and shoots. If they can establish a healthy canopy first, they'll deliver a better harvest the following season and beyond.

So, while you don't have to, it's advisable to take this step for your patch of June-bearers their first season. Diligently snip off flower buds at the base. For the other types—day-neutrals, everbearers, and even the alpines—remove flower buds and runners only through early July of the first year. Allow them to set fruit from then on.

HARVESTING AND AFTERCARE

Plucking fresh, aromatic strawberries for yourself and your family is great fun. But there are some things you should know, about how and when to pick, as well as the best way to care for the plants after the harvest period is over, so they'll keep on producing for you in years to come.

Picking

Generally speaking, strawberries are ripe 28 to 30 days after full bloom, and should be harvested every two to three days—daily in hot weather, or, in cooler climates, less often. (See the table on page 59 for typical harvest times.) Use the taste test, or pick berries when they are fully colored. Ideally, do this in the morning, after the plants have dried, to maximize their shelf life. Prolong shelf life further by leaving on the green caps.

Some gardeners take a colander or a basket into the garden and gently set the berries in as they work their way through the bed. Another good method is to line a shallow plastic container with paper towels (to absorb excess moisture), placing a fresh new sheet between each layer to a depth of about four layers.

Keep picked berries out of direct sun, and refrigerate them as soon as possible. Do not wash or hull them until just prior to use.

Renovation of June-bearers

Thinning, narrowing, and mowing your June-bearing strawberry beds—a process known as renovation—invigorates the plants and helps them produce larger fruit. Beds that retain too many plants end up yielding fewer, small berries that are difficult to find under the dense foliage. (*Do not renovate day-neutral and everbearing strawberries.* You should expect to replace plants of these two types regularly—every year or two.)

Begin immediately after harvest of your June-bearers is completed. This timing gives the plants a chance to grow a new canopy of leaves, which will, come fall, determine the amount and quality of the flower buds that will produce fruit the following spring.

Renovation entails removing weeds, narrowing rows to 6 to 12 inches (15 to 30 cm), and thinning the plants to one plant about every 5 inches (13 cm) or so in the row. In large plantings, you can accomplish row-narrowing with a rototiller; use a shovel or trowel in a small planting.

As you work the bed, try to select for the strongest runner (daughter) plants. Remove mother plants altogether, as they are unproductive. Clip or mow leaves down using a mower, weed-whacker (string trimmer), or, if your patch is small, shears. Don't scalp, but reduce the plants to about 1½ inches (4 cm) high. Then, fertilize the plants with your favorite organic plant food or with about 5 pounds (2 kg) of balanced 10-10-10 fertilizer per 100 feet (30 m) of row. Finally, water well.

If renovation is done properly, your first response should be, "Oh my gosh! What have I done?" The planting will look completely devastated, and you will wonder how it will ever recover. Again, take heart. Continue to water and tend to the needs of the planting, and you will be amazed at the vigor with which it rebounds.

Overwintering
Unless you live in a mild climate such as the Pacific Northwest, you should mulch your strawberry plants every late fall. (Pacific Northwest gardeners should not, as mulch combined with mild and wet winters makes plantings waterlogged and will lead to poor plant health.) This helps protect them from the cold, prevents frost-heaving (which can happen when there are sudden drops in temperature), and prevents bud break from occurring too early in the spring.

Use a clean, weed-free mulch, of course, such as wheat, oat, or rye straw. Apply it liberally, to a depth of approximately 4 inches (10 cm) over the tops of the plants just before the snow flies. Be careful that it doesn't clump, which can smother plants.

Remove mulch from the tops of the plants in spring after the danger of severe cold has passed but before much leaf yellowing on the new growth occurs. Scoot some or all of it into the center of the rows. There, it provides a bed on which your upcoming season's berries can ripen.

Please note that strawberry flower buds and fruit are susceptible to frost injury any time after bud break. In areas with late frosts, a crop can be substantially damaged even after the berries are developing. Early-blooming cultivars are more likely to be injured by frost than late cultivars, of course. If a late frost is forecast, get out there the afternoon before and spread several layers of newspaper or old blankets on

Cold, frosty weather signals the end of the strawberry season. If you garden in a cold region and plan to carry your plants over for next season, be sure to lay down an ample mulch.

the planting. Or purchase a frost blanket and keep it around for this purpose.

Frost damage typically results in flowers with black centers, rather than yellow ones; frost-damaged flowers will not develop into fruit. Occasionally frost will damage only a portion of a flower. This portion will not develop properly, so the berry will look lopsided. But you can still eat and enjoy it, and congratulate yourself on the barely escaped fruit-killing frost.

TROUBLESHOOTING

While your strawberry patch can stay healthy and provide delicious fruit if you follow the good practices outlined in this chapter, there may be no avoiding some problems. Observe and diagnose correctly before attempting control measures. General information about ways to manage common troubles are in this book's first chapter—take time to review that material. The following are problems and recommendations specific to strawberries.

Fungal diseases

Strawberries are vulnerable to a whole host of fungal diseases that will injure or kill them. Fortunately, plant breeders have helped us out considerably by developing many resistant cultivars. You can help yourself, too, by purchasing and growing disease-resistant plants whenever possible; refer to a reputable nursery's catalog for information on disease-resistant cultivars.

You can further help your situation by

Oh no! Rot on your beautiful berries?! Take the time to discover the cause before trying to treat any such problem.

The dreaded gray mold ruins berries for eating and can spread in a planting, so be on the lookout. This problem is easier to prevent than to treat.

being picky about where you plant strawberries. If puddles of water remain on the site after a light rain, you are almost guaranteed to have root-rot problems. The site you select must be well drained. If you do not have any suitable sites, remember that strawberries grow quite nicely in raised beds as well as in a variety of containers including strawberry pots and pyramids—for more details, refer back to "Strawberries in Containers" on page 70.

Gray mold (pathogen: *Botrytis cinerea*) is by far the most troublesome and common disease. This fuzzy mold forms on ripe berries and, in extreme conditions, on green fruit as well. Spores infect the plant in blossom and lie dormant in the developing berries until fruit sugars are high enough to encourage the spores to grow and eventually produce even more spores on the ripe fruit. These infect

other ripening fruit from the outside (called a secondary infection), and so on and so on.

The time when the plants are blooming is critical. Chances are if you have dry weather during this period, you will not have much trouble with gray mold. If you see a fruit with mold on it in your planting, get it out of there! As you harvest, you will inevitably miss a few ripe berries, and these may become infected and threaten other fruit. Picking that rotten fruit and disposing of it in the compost pile is a nasty job, but force yourself to do it and you should be able to control the disease.

Another good technique for controlling gray mold is to make sure that the plants are not too dense in a strawberry patch. A density of about one plant every 5 inches (13 cm) is optimal. If your plants are closer than that, they take longer to dry after rain or irrigation, making a great environment for the fungus. Gray mold develops when free water is about, so anything you can do to reduce drying time and increase air circulation also helps. Evidence also suggests that excessive nitrogen applied during the growing season will predispose the fruit to gray mold.

Anthracnose in strawberries is attributed to various fungal pathogens (*Colletotrichum* spp.). Warm, humid weather encourages it; it tends not to be an issue in cooler, drier growing conditions. Watch out for dark lesions developing on the leaves; browned, dying and dead blossoms; and sunken dark spots on fruit. Tear out and destroy affected plants. The best preventative is a resistant cultivar.

Red stele and **verticillium wilt** are common diseases of the strawberry, but they are rarely a serious problem for the home gardener—provided that the right site and cultivars are selected and good cultural practices are used. Red stele (pathogen: *Phytophthora fragariae*) will be a problem only in wet sites with heavy soils; even so, resistant cultivars can sometimes overcome these negatives. Verticillium wilt (pathogen: *Verticillium* spp.) can be completely avoided by not planting your strawberries where this fungus has harmed other susceptible plants (black raspberries, tomatoes, potatoes, eggplants). Though some resistant cultivars are available, verticillium resistance is not nearly as reliable as red stele resistance. Symptoms of both diseases include weak growth and often the complete collapse of the plant.

Leather rot (pathogen: *Phytophthora cactorum*) is another rot disease that might occur in years when spring and early summer are especially rainy and damp. It attacks both green and ripe berries. Affected green ones become brown, with a rough, leathery texture; affected mature ones discolor, soften, and taste bitter. Cull diseased berries and debris around your plants and throw it all away; harvest often and early, in the morning after dew has dried. Straw mulch that shields your berries from direct contact with the soil is a good preventative, as is, of course, sufficient light, good air circulation, and a well-drained site.

Powdery mildew (pathogen: *Podosphaera aphanis*) is usually not a problem on strawberry fruit, but it may infect leaves in years that are especially damp or foggy in the spring and dry in the summer. This fungal disease is trouble if it occurs in the fall and limits plant photosynthesis. Since flower bud initiation takes place in the fall, if the plant is unable to photosynthesize due to the disease, then of course its ability to form next year's flower buds will be limited. All this can be avoided by appropriate site selection—don't plant in low-lying areas, which are subject to poor air circulation and vulnerable to frost.

Leaf spot, while not fatal, detracts from the look of your patch and weakens plants; productivity can decline.

Strawberry leaf spot (pathogen: *Mycosphaerella fragariae*) used to be more common and is still an occasional problem for home growers, but the good news is that most modern-day cultivars are resistant. Leaf spots appear brown with purple edges, and they expand. Berries can also become discolored. Warm, humid weather tends to bring it on. Good cultural practices and resistant cultivars are your best preventatives.

Common pests and other problems

Fortunately, insects and other pests that seriously injure strawberry plants on a regular basis are few. The primary threats are discussed here.

Tarnished plant bug (*Lygus* spp.) can lurk in strawberries and cause damage from bloom time all the way through fruiting. A relative of the stinkbug, only smaller, the tarnished plant bug has for a mouth a long needle-like protuberance, which it injects into the blossom or the developing fruit, slurping out the contents and deforming the fruit. This deformation usually occurs on the tip of the berry, giving it a button-like, nubby appearance and seedy texture. It does not hurt the fruit in any other way—the fruit is still edible and tasty—and so some folks opt to ignore the deformed fruit.

If it gets bad enough, though, the damage from tarnished plant bug can take a bite out of your production. These pests are known to overwinter in weedy areas, so mowing nearby weedy areas might help. Some gardeners fight back by putting the white sticky boards that orchardists use around the strawberry patch.

Sap beetles (*Stelidota geminata*) simply love ripe strawberries. These little black beetles are especially attracted to fruit that has been damaged by birds or slugs. The best preventative is to keep the fruit well harvested, something you probably intended to do anyway. As with gray mold, removing overripe fruit from the planting will improve control. Since the odor of the rotting fruit is what attracts sap beetles in the first place, it's been suggested that by placing an old container of rotting fruit far from your strawberry patch, you can lure the beetles away from the planting. It's worth a try if you have a lot of these pests in your area, but keeping the plot well picked should be sufficient.

Strawberry root weevil (*Otiorhynchus ovatus*) can show up in late spring. Suspect them when you notice ragged chewed edges on young leaves. While this won't kill your strawberry plants, the worse is yet to come if you don't act. Their life cycle will proceed to the point where adults lay eggs in your patch, and the resulting larvae (white, C-shaped) expand the damage. They'll dine on roots and crowns, which stunts growth, reduces yields, and eventually can kill the plants. So intervene in spring. The weevils—which cannot fly—eat at night, so go out to the patch with a flashlight and knock the ¼ inch (0.5 cm) pests off the plants into a box or onto a carefully towed sheet or tarp, then kill them. If you waited too long, tear out

afflicted plants, dispose of them, and yank out or mow down the patch at season's end, with the goal of either solarizing the area, turning it over to a cover crop, or starting over in another part of the yard.

Strawberry clipper or **strawberry bud weevil** (*Anthonomus signatus*) damages the plant by laying eggs in a stem in the flowering cluster, causing the stem to break and killing the flower. If you see several broken stems in your planting before bloom, you have likely been hit by the strawberry clipper, although you will rarely see the offending insect. Older literature recommends insecticide sprays for control, but more recent research has found that, though individual fruits are lost, the plant compensates somewhat by developing new flowers or by increasing the size of the remaining fruit. Probably the best approach is to simply wait and see how the crop develops.

Spotted wing drosophila (*Drosophila suzukii*)—SWD for short—is a type of vinegar fly (they look quite similar to fruit flies). This small fly is increasingly a problem on various fruit crops, especially raspberries and blueberries. It can also attack strawberries but is mostly a problem on the day-neutrals, not the June-bearers. When it gets into your day-neutrals, the fruit rots and literally melts down, often followed by mold—a real mess. Commercial growers spray for these, but

Slug damage is not hard to spot. Even if you don't see their shiny, slimy trails, you'll find the large bites they've taken out of your precious fruit.

home gardeners are advised to just take preventive steps. Keep your fruit picked, and remove and get rid of old and affected fruit. (For more details, please consult the description in the blueberry chapter.)

Slugs and snails. These pests are a problem only in rainy years, unless you live in slug-infested territory like the Pacific Northwest. In most climates, the weather eliminates slugs as a threat for about a third of the growing season. But when slugs are a problem, they are *really* a problem. They eat holes in ripe or nearly ripe fruit, usually at the cap end of the fruit and often on the underside as well if fruit is lying on the ground, leaving telltale cavities. Slugs can also provide entry holes for sap beetles and other pests. And one of the worst harvesting experiences has to be picking up a large, fully ripe strawberry from the patch and seeing not only a large hole on the bottom but also the slimy culprit that caused it slithering along the fruit.

Slugs are attracted to beer, so setting out small tin cans or pie plates filled halfway with beer will trap a lot of these mucilaginous pests. Marvin Pritts at Cornell University found that slugs were more attracted to expensive, imported beers than to run-of-the-mill brews—interesting! Diatomaceous earth is purported to be a slug killer—supposedly slicing their bodies as they crawl over it—but its effectiveness is questionable. As a last resort, you can scatter slug baits made with iron phosphate around your planting site.

Birds. Though they can decimate a blueberry planting, birds don't often spell serious trouble for strawberries. Netting is the best approach if birds (robins and starlings are usually the worst offenders) are taking more than their share. Spread the netting loosely over the planting, weighing the edges down to keep birds from getting underneath.

Weeds. The strawberry plant is particularly sensitive to competition from weeds because it is short (so taller plants can easily block

Should birds start going after your strawberries, protect the plants with a loose covering of netting or chicken wire—anything that keeps them out but still allows the necessities of light, air, and water in. Don't forget to anchor down the sides so the winged munchers can't hop under.

Don't give weeds an inch! These pesky, aggressive plants will compete with your strawberries not only for garden space but for moisture and nutrients—and the berry plants may lose. Be diligent about yanking them out the moment you spot them.

its light) and shallow-rooted (so it does not compete well for water and soil nutrients). The only cure is to be vigilant about weeding. The most problematic time for new growers is at planting, before the plants have filled in their area, because nature loves to fill in bare soil. Keep on top of the problem. Going through the planting and pulling weeds once a week is ideal, but you definitely should get in there at least every two weeks.

STRAWBERRIES ARE BELOVED for good reason—beautiful, sweetly fragrant, delicious, and they grow well almost everywhere. While the information in this chapter may seem like a lot to absorb, the upshot is that it's really not that difficult to raise healthy, productive plants that will be an asset to any landscape. Find a cultivar recommended for your growing conditions, choose a spot that's sunny and not damp, and get started. Once your strawberries are up and growing, you have a lot to look forward to—just imagine the delight and pride you'll feel, the great breakfasts, jams, and desserts you can enjoy!

raspberries and
blackberries

SWEET BUT NOT TOO, STIMULATING BUT

not brash, full of heavenly aroma: raspberries and blackberries truly rank as foods fit for the gods. And it's no secret: they are highly satisfying to mere mortals, too. These robust plants, which require little in the way of pest control or maintenance when appropriately sited, are tempting candidates for homegrown berries, even if you have only a small backyard. A 10-foot (3-m) row of raspberry plants, for example, gives you enough berries to eat in season, plus surplus to freeze or turn into jam. What a great holiday present—bright red raspberry jam that tastes like it just came out of the garden, just as winter's darkness is starting to descend.

Although they are lanky growers, it is entirely possible, with careful siting and training, to add a handful of raspberry plants to your yard. Then you'll get to enjoy their benefits— wonderful fruit plus a natural, living screen of foliage.

As the saying goes, good fences make good neighbors. All too true! And raspberry and blackberry hedges stand ready to help you improve relationships with those living in close proximity to you. The summer-bearing raspberries will have a constant presence once established, whereas the fall-bearers can be kept year-round (fruiting in fall and summer) or mowed so that the hedge "disappears" during the dormant season, only to grow up again in the summer. Fall-bearing red raspberries fit in well with ornamental plantings of bleeding hearts, peonies, and other spring-flowering plants that tend to die off or look ratty as the summer progresses. The perennials will just be finishing up as the raspberries get going.

If you want berries but not thorns, such plants exist. Thornless blackberries can be trained to any structure, including existing fences that are less than 8 feet (2.5 m) in height. You must, however, tie their canes to the structure, since they do not have tendrils (as, say, grapes do) with which to attach themselves.

If you want berry plants that do double

Left to their own devices, blackberries grow quite tall and broad over time, and their thorns can be forbidding. And yet—the berries are delicious: it was inevitable that people would intervene to make selections and improvements so these tasty treats could be enjoyed more easily.

duty as a prickly fence or property line, however, thorny erect blackberries make a hedge that is daunting to intruders or trespassers. Just bear in mind that these plants sucker from the root system, and you should disclose this to your neighbors. Let them know that they can mow down suckers that come up on their property (this is probably the easiest control) and that they are welcome to harvest berries from their side of the hedge—such an offer should more than make up for the inconvenience.

A bramble is defined as any plant belonging to the genus *Rubus*. The best-known ones are raspberries and blackberries (or, as they are collectively known in the West, caneberries). Several types of raspberries and blackberries are widely grown, and hybrids between the two (tayberries, boysenberries, loganberries) are produced on a limited scale; a bit of information on these less-common types is ahead in this chapter, if you are interested.

The red raspberry (*Rubus idaeus*), native to most of the temperate regions of the world (including North America), has been cultivated in Europe for centuries. Another North American native, the black raspberry

(*R. occidentalis*), has been domesticated only since the mid-1800s. Purple raspberries were recognized as hybrids between red and black raspberries as early as 1870; plants display hybrid vigor, but their berries usually lack the sweetness of the two parent species.

As to the blackberry, early European settlers in North America viewed the various species more as weeds than as potential crops. Great effort was put into killing the plants, although it's also likely that berries were gathered from wild stands and put to good use. Although blackberries were domesticated in Europe by the 1600s, they were not cultivated by North Americans until the 1800s. Once they were, refinements were made. Nowadays, blackberries are generally grouped into three main types: erect, semi-erect, and trailing.

Erect and semi-erect blackberries were developed from eastern North American wild species; they are very similar in fruit characteristics but have a few notable plant differences. Erect blackberries (if not tipped) will grow 6 to 10 feet (1.8 to 3 m) tall, sucker profusely from the roots like red raspberry, have moderate to good cold hardiness, have thorny and thornless cultivars, and respond to summer tipping of the primocanes with increased yield the following year. Semi-erect blackberries (if not tipped) will grow to 15 feet (4.5 m), are crown-forming (no suckers), have moderate cold hardiness,

have only thornless cultivars, and also respond to summer tipping.

The trailing types were developed from western blackberry species, with a good dose of red raspberry. The fruit of trailing blackberries differs from that of their eastern-developed counterparts: berries tend to have less noticeable seeds, tend to be conic rather than round in shape, and ripen earlier. Also—gardeners and pie-bakers take note—the berries have more intense flavors, with high levels of sugar and acid. Trailing blackberry plants do not respond to tipping; their canes will grow 10 to 20 feet (3 to 6 m) long, are crown-forming (no suckers), have poor to moderate cold hardiness, and have thornless and thorny cultivars.

In the past few years a new type of blackberry has been developed from erect blackberries. These fall-bearing/primocane-fruiting blackberries (for example, 'Prime-Ark 45') are similar to the fall-bearing/primocane-fruiting raspberries in that they fruit on the current season's growth and can then be cut to the ground in the winter. Their fruit is comparable to other erect blackberries.

ABOUT THE PLANT

Rubus species typically have perennial roots and crowns, but the canes are biennial, living only for two summers. This is why you

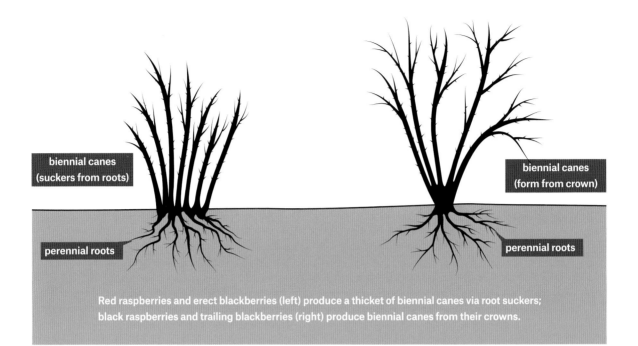

biennial canes
(suckers from roots)

biennial canes
(form from crown)

perennial roots

perennial roots

Red raspberries and erect blackberries (left) produce a thicket of biennial canes via root suckers;
black raspberries and trailing blackberries (right) produce biennial canes from their crowns.

don't tend to get a crop until the second year after planting. This is also why you have to intervene with your clippers (and protective gloves) to keep the plants from becoming congested with old canes and to encourage optimum berry production.

Here's how they work. The green vegetative shoots that grow in the first season are called primocanes. They overwinter, and in their second year, now referred to as floricanes, they become mature (browner). The floricanes then leaf out, flower, fruit, and die during the second growing season.

While the floricanes are going through flowering, fruiting, and dying, the plant's root system is simultaneously putting out new primocanes. These in turn will provide the fruit for the following year. The exceptions to this life cycle are the fall-bearing (also known as primocane-fruiting or

everbearing) red raspberries, black raspberries, and blackberries, which produce canes, flower, and fruit in a single season and do not die after first fruiting.

Each *Rubus* fruit is composed of many individual sections called drupelets. The drupelets are loosely held together by intertwining hairs at the base of the fruit, as well as by a waxy deposit on the surface.

Finally, raspberries and blackberries are self-fertile, meaning that you don't need extra plants or different cultivars in order to get a harvest.

RASPBERRY TYPES

Red (includes yellow), black, and purple raspberries are the three most commonly grown raspberry types. The word "types" is used intentionally, because the difference

BRAMBLE FRUIT DETAIL.

BERRY DIFFERENCES

The main difference between raspberries and blackberries is how they separate from the plant when harvested ripe. Raspberry fruits detach from the receptacle, resulting in a fruit with a cup-shaped cavity where it was previously attached to the plant. In blackberry fruits, by contrast, the receptacle—appearing as a center of white tissue inside the fruit—is consumed as part of the fruit; the "plug" of tissue in the center of blackberries helps prevent crushing, which is one reason their shelf life is slightly longer than that of raspberries. This imperfect differentiation between the two bramble fruits leads to the uncomfortable fact that boysenberries and loganberries, which are very purple or red, are classified as blackberries.

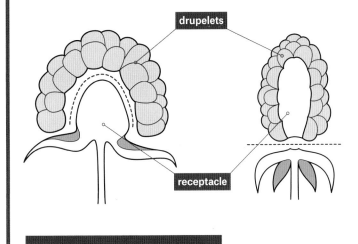

Raspberry (left) and blackberry (right), with dashed lines indicating abscission (fruit removal) zone.

among them is not only the color of the fruit but also the growth habit (and hence the cultural practices), pest susceptibility, and other characteristics. Raspberry plants range in height from about thigh-high, such as some of the more cold-hardy types grown in New England, to 8 to 10 feet (2.5 to 3 m) tall in the Pacific Northwest. Leaves are usually composed of three (sometimes five) leaflets, are light to medium green in color, and have serrated edges. The plants are generally considered hardy in zones (3)4 to 8.

Red raspberries

Red (includes yellow) raspberries (*Rubus idaeus*) are further divided into two categories, summer-bearing and fall-bearing. Summer-bearing red raspberries have the typical biennial life cycle of a bramble: fruit is borne only on the second-year canes (mid-July to August harvest in most regions) and the canes die after fruiting. Fall-bearing red raspberries, however, fruit during the first year on the new canes. They produce the bulk of their luscious fruit in late summer through fall (August to October in most regions). Fruiting ceases at the first hard frost; they will fruit again in spring, on the buds closer to the base of the plant than the last buds that fruited the previous fall.

Yellow- to gold-fruited raspberries are simply a fruit color mutation; they are treated exactly like any other red raspberry.

Black raspberries

Black raspberries (*Rubus occidentalis*) usually bear their dark purple to black fruit slightly earlier in the season (mid-June to

Yellow raspberries, a type of red raspberry, are sought after for their mild, sweet flavor.

Ever notice how raspberry fruits have tiny little hairs on them? These hairs are what's left of the pistils (the female parts) of the flower after the petals fall and the fruit begins to form. Blackberries, which are otherwise fairly similar, lack them.

MEET THE HYBRID BLACKBERRIES

The pedigrees of all trailing blackberries trace to several *Rubus* species, although the western dewberry (*Rubus ursinus*) dominates. Raspberry is also common, in large part because the blackberry × raspberry hybrid 'Logan' was so frequently used as a parent in breeding programs. A few retain some raspberry characteristics, including boysenberries, tayberries, and the more recently released 'Newberry'. All are considered blackberries, no matter their color, because when they are harvested, the receptacle (core) picks with the fruit.

Boysenberry fruits are large, soft, and deep maroon, with a distinctive and excellent flavor sought after by gourmets. Canes are quite thorny.

Loganberry fruits are medium in size, soft, elongated, and dark red. They have good flavor. Most are thorny.

'Newberry' is a relatively new hybrid. Its tasty fruit is bigger than that of 'Marion', and the color is more purple than black. The habit is trailing and yes, the plant is thorny.

Tayberry fruits are deep red, elongated, glossy, and have a distinctive flavor that is prized for pies and used to make a beautiful ruby-red jam. Unfortunately, they are extremely difficult to pick.

mid-July in most regions) and are more cold-tender than the hardiest of the red raspberries. They further differ from red raspberries in initiating new canes from the crown of the plant rather than from root suckers; therefore, they are grown in a hill system, in which each plant is grown independently, with pruning and maintenance done on a per-plant basis.

Unlike red raspberries, black raspberries require summer tipping (see "Pruning," page 113), to encourage branching that leads to more flower buds and a bigger crop. In the fall, their shoots tend to begin to dive toward the ground, forming what growers call "rat tails." Where these touch the ground, they root and form plants (this is called tip layering). This is a major maintenance problem, unless you want a bigger planting. Control this potential weediness by trimming off the rat tails (rooted and unrooted) late in the fall.

Recently 'Niwot' and 'Explorer' primocane-fruiting black raspberries were released. These behave like the fall-bearing raspberries in that they fruit on the current

'Olallie', a thorny trailing blackberry selection, in bloom.

season's growth. More are in the pipeline; if this sort of plant intrigues you, check with your nursery source.

Purple raspberries

Purple raspberries are hybrids between red and black raspberries and are intermediate between the parent species in hardiness. They bear fruit from late June to late July in most regions. New canes are initiated predominantly from the crown, but suckers may form between plants as well. Grow these in the same manner as black raspberries.

BLACKBERRY TYPES

Blackberry canes are very vigorous and generally larger than those of raspberries. Their thorns are, shall we say, more significant than raspberry thorns; however, many of the new cultivars are thornless. All blackberries are rated hardy in zones 5 to 7(8), but

BLACKBERRY CANES EXPLAINED

There are two types of canes, primocanes and floricanes. Understanding this will help you better care for your plants and follow pruning advice.

- Primocanes are first-year canes. Most blackberry types produce no fruit on these; you have to wait till the second year.
- Floricanes are primocanes in their second year of growth. These develop flowers, fruit, and then die.

this can vary by type and cultivar, so be sure to double-check if you are concerned about plants making it through your winters.

Erect blackberries

Erect blackberries can have excellent fruit quality. Both thorny and thornless cultivars

TYPICAL BRAMBLE HARVEST TIMES

	Summer-bearing raspberries	Fall-bearing raspberries	Blackberries
Northeast	mid-July–August	late August–October	July–September*
Southeast	March–June	June–September	April–early June
Midwest	mid-July–August	late August–October	July–September*
Rocky Mountain	mid-July–August	late August–October	July–September
Northwest	mid-June	mid-August–frost	late June–frost
Southwest	[too warm]	June–frost	May–August

* Summer-bearing blackberries are not recommended for colder parts of
  New England and the upper Midwest because of low winter temperatures.

are available, but the former are slowly disappearing from cultivation because the thorns present such an obstacle to managing and harvesting. Like rose thorns, these recurve: if they don't get you going in, they'll get you coming out. So, unless you are planting to make a barrier, choose one of the outstanding thornless cultivars. Though less cold-tolerant than many raspberries, erect blackberries are hardier than the semi-erect or trailing types.

Plants are 4 to 12 feet (1.2 to 4 m) in height, usually, so you'll need to give them some support to keep the canes from falling over. Most produce fruit on floricanes, generally from early July to late August. They respond to summer tipping (see "Pruning," page 113), and, like raspberries, they produce root suckers.

Primocane-fruiting erect blackberries, pioneered by breeders at the University of Arkansas (and given cultivar names that begin with "Prime-"), are a newer type in this category. They flower and fruit in their first season, producing fruit on the tips of their primocanes (similar to fall-bearing raspberries). When they are about 3 feet (1 m) tall, they should be tipped to 2 feet (0.6 m) tall; removing one-third instead of just a couple inches seems drastic, but it has been shown to lead to a bigger crop. If left

to overwinter, the part of the primocane that didn't fruit will become a floricane and flower (and fruit) the following summer—thus, you can get two crops per year: the first, in midsummer, on floricanes; the second, in autumn, on new primocanes.

Despite being developed in the upper South, primocane-fruiting erect blackberries are not well adapted there; when flowering takes place in the heat of the summer, the flowers have very poor set. Also, they are too late for most northern climates. The upshot is that they are best for areas with more moderate summer temperatures and a long growing season. So far, these aren't extremely productive, but better and earlier cultivars are sure to come along.

Hardiness is not important for erect blackberries because you mow the canes to the ground each year and new ones emerge each spring, regardless of how cold the winter was.

Semi-erect blackberries
Semi-erect blackberries grow to 15 feet (4.5 m), and the long canes arch to the ground when not supported. These are crown-forming and respond to summer tipping, with increased branching and therefore yield the following year. All cultivars are thornless.

SCORN THORNS?

If you are interested in growing brambles but really dislike dealing with prickles and thorns while pruning and during harvesting, good news: most new cultivars don't have them. But before you get too enthused, verify that your choice will do well in your hardiness zone/region. Some thornless plants are less cold-hardy than their highly armed counterparts. As for flavor, it's a matter of taste.

In raspberries, try 'Joan J', available from specialty nurseries. Or seek out BrazelBerries® 'Raspberry Shortcake', a dwarf thornless introduction from Monrovia; at only 2 to 3 feet (0.6 to 1 m) tall, this novelty raspberry can be grown in a big container.

In blackberries, look for 'Black Diamond', 'Chester Thornless', 'Columbia Star', 'Loch Ness', 'Natchez', 'Navaho', 'Ouachita', and 'Triple Crown'. There are thornless boysenberries and loganberries, but their fruit quality is considered inferior to their thorny counterparts.

Not only does 'Chester Thornless' produce delicious blackberries, it has pretty pale pink flowers and, of course, friendly canes.

Trailing blackberries

Trailing blackberries grow 10 to 20 feet (3 to 6 m) along the ground and must be lifted up and supported on wires or a hefty trellis—a fair amount of work for a home gardener to consider. They are crown-forming, do not respond to summer tipping, and bear fruit from mid-June to late August. Fruit tends to be cone-shaped, with much less noticeable seeds. Flavor is intense, thanks to high sugar and acid content. Again, anyone looking to make jams or syrups, or to freeze their blackberry crop, take note!

These are tender, with only poor to moderate cold hardiness, and are mostly raised from California into British Columbia, primarily along the coast, and in the Southeast. When planted in these mild climates, trailing blackberries are by far the earliest ripening types, fruiting two to three weeks ahead of the others. Their early ripening and the fact that they can be left on the ground is being taken advantage of by Midwest growers, who place row covers over the canes on the ground, overwinter them, and then in spring raise them up. In this way, they can have the earliest fruit on the market. Several trailing blackberries are thorny, but their spines are more comparable to raspberry spines than the sharper spines of eastern blackberries.

CHOOSING THE RIGHT CULTIVAR

Selecting appropriate and disease-resistant cultivars is an important decision. You'll want to consult with neighbors, local Cooperative Extension personnel, and local

KEY TO REGIONS

NE = Northeast, including southern Quebec and southern Ontario

SE = Southeast, including Gulf Coast

MW = Midwest and Great Plains, including adjacent Canadian provinces

RM = Rocky Mountain/Mountain West

NW = Pacific Northwest, including Northern California and British Columbia

SW = Southwest and Southern California

'Canby'

nurseries for the most up-to-date information on cultivars for your location. How the berries taste is also an essential question! If you are unsure, plant a few plants, fruit them for a couple of years, and replant if you don't like them. Testing is part of the journey—and getting there is half the fun.

With some red raspberry cultivars, it seems that size and taste have an inverse relationship. A classic biggie, 'Titan', has a mild (not to say bland) flavor. On the other hand, though fruit size is smaller, good old 'Heritage' is hard to beat among the fall-bearing types for flavor and output. And raspberry flavor will vary from location to location; 'Heritage', for example, tastes great when grown in loam or clay loam, but its flavor is diminished in sandier soils.

Black raspberries are more flavorful than the reds, although they also tend to be seedier. Recent research shows that most cultivars are very closely related (or, in fact, the same!), so it's not surprising to find little variation in flavor from cultivar to cultivar. Upshot: go for size with black raspberries.

The seediness of blackberries may be an issue for you, something to bear in mind when shopping. Those that seem the least seedy are the trailing types ('Black Diamond', 'Columbia Star', 'Marion'). If you like

a sweet berry, then a fully ripe 'Navaho', 'Ouachita', or 'Triple Crown' is a great choice. If you like a blackberry that has a full sweet-acid balance and is terrific when processed, you may want to grow 'Boysen', 'Columbia Star', or 'Marion'.

Growth habit remains an issue with blackberries. Erect and semi-erect ones are easier to manage than the lanky-stemmed trailing ones. So read the cultivar descriptions carefully to balance this against the sort of berry you want to eat.

Use the recommendations in the cultivar lists as guidelines only: your particular growing region or microclimates in your own yard may allow you to explore beyond those listed.

Summer-bearing raspberries

'Boyne' NE RM NW Early. Very cold hardy and productive. Berries are dark red, small to medium in size. Plants are short.

'Canby' NE MW RM NW Early. Moderately cold hardy and nearly thornless. Plants are productive, with attractive, medium to large, bright red fruit. Susceptible to root rot.

'Tulameen'

'Willamette'

'Cascade Bounty' NW Midseason. Productive with medium-sized, bright red fruit that is a bit unevenly shaped. Especially root-rot resistant.

'Cascade Delight' NW Mid to late season. Vigorous and productive. Very large, beautiful, well-colored, firm fruit with outstanding flavor. Plants have good tolerance to root rot.

'Chemainus' NW Midseason. Very productive with medium-sized, bright red, easily harvested fruit with excellent flavor.

'Dormanred' SE Midseason. Developed from *Rubus parvifolius* rather than the typical red raspberry, so while it is well adapted to hot climates, the fruit flavor is very different—some people like it; others do not. It is, however, one of the few raspberries that survives the heat of the South.

'Killarney' NE NW Early. Fruit is medium-sized and bright red. Productive, hardy, and well armed with spines. Produces many suckers. Like its sibling 'Boyne', the plant is short.

'Latham' NE MW NW Late. Excellent cold hardiness. Plant is susceptible to mildew but resists viruses fairly well. Fruit size is small to medium, flavor is acceptable, firmness is good. Relatively long bearing season. Old standard eastern cultivar.

'Malahat' NW Very early. Fruit is large, firm, bright red, and has excellent flavor. Plant has moderate productivity but unfortunately is susceptible to root rot.

'Meeker' NW Midseason. Firm, medium to large fruit with good flavor. Ripens later than 'Willamette'. Very productive in the Pacific Northwest but susceptible to winter injury. Less productive in hot areas of California.

'Nova' NE MW RM Midseason. Berries are medium-sized and firm. Flavor is somewhat acidic. Plants have good vigor and few thorns. Very hardy. Can be raised for primocane crop only.

'Prelude' NE MW NW Very early. The earliest summer-bearing raspberry available—it fruits during strawberry season. Hardiness and flavor are good. It will also produce a small crop in fall on primocanes.

'Saanich' NW Midseason. Productive with medium-sized, bright red, easily harvested fruit with excellent flavor.

'Anne'

'Autumn Bliss'

'Autumn Britten'

'Taylor' NE MW Late. Medium fruit size, good flavor, and moderate cold hardiness. Susceptible to mosaic virus and fungal diseases.

'Titan' NE MW Midseason. A productive cultivar with very large, soft, cone-shaped berries with a mild (approaching bland) taste. Plants have excellent vigor but moderate cold hardiness. Resistant to the raspberry aphid but particularly susceptible to phytophthora root rot, so make sure soil is especially well drained.

'Tulameen' SE NW Early. Produces very large fruit that is firm and bright red, with excellent flavor. Poor cold hardiness and extremely susceptible to root rot.

'Willamette' NW Early. Medium to large fruit, dark red with mild flavor. Susceptible to root rot, and not productive in heavy (clay) soils. Long considered the standard summer-bearer for the Pacific Northwest. Less productive in hot areas of California.

Fall-bearing raspberries

'Amity' NW Early. Small to medium fruit, firm, dark red, with outstanding flavor. Moderately productive. Good for freezing.

'Anne' (yellow) NE MW RM NW SW Late. A medium to tall plant that produces very few primocanes, limiting its yield. Not thornless, but definitely a lower thorn count than some others. Fruit is a true yellow, large, slightly rough in appearance. The wonderful flavor has overtones of banana; the flavor improves as the season progresses. Worth growing for the unusual and delicious jam it makes.

'Autumn Bliss' NE MW NW Early. A vigorous plant. Berries are large and have excellent flavor. Canes are of large diameter and medium height; they tend to sucker in clumps around the original plants. Ripens considerably earlier than 'Heritage', though fruit quality is not as consistent.

'Autumn Britten' NE MW RM NW Early to midseason. Medium height and good productivity. Ripens later in the season than 'Autumn Bliss' but still earlier than 'Heritage'. Fruit size and quality are good at the beginning but diminish as the season progresses.

'Bababerry' SW Early. Berries are large, sweet, and firm. An excellent choice for hot regions with mild winters. Can be hard to find, however.

'Caroline'

'Caroline' NE SE MW RM NW SW Midseason. High-yielding, excellently flavored fruit, though berries can be rough in appearance. Strong raspberry taste. Cane height varies considerably, with the shorter canes bearing earlier in the season than the taller ones. Not as thorny as some others. An excellent choice for California gardeners.

'Cascade Gold' (yellow) NW Midseason. Large fruit with outstanding flavor. Plants are vigorous and productive but susceptible to root rot.

'Crimson Giant' NE MW Late. Moderate yields of very large, mild-flavored, firm berries that can be a bit rough.

'Fallgold' (yellow) NE MW Late. An older cultivar with medium-sized fruit. Texture is quite soft, but flavor is incredible, holding up even in hot summers. Also quite cold-hardy, producing late into autumn.

'Goldie' (yellow) NE MW Midseason. A yellow mutation of 'Heritage', comparable in all ways except fruit color. Fruit is prone to sun-bleaching and is actually more of a pink or orange by the time it is (easily) removed from the receptacle.

'Heritage' NE SE MW RM NW SW Late. Medium-sized, firm fruit of excellent quality. Hardy fruit tolerates light frosts well. Plants are very vigorous and sucker well. The standard among fall-bearers, its only limitation being that it begins bearing too late for the northernmost climes.

'Honey Queen' (yellow) MW RM Mid to late season. Quite cold-hardy, developed in Alberta, Canada. Berries are on the larger side, with a honey-sweet flavor. Thinner, longer canes tend to flop on the ground so must be supported and tied.

'Josephine' SW Late. Large, bright-red firm fruit with excellent flavor. Good vigor and productivity.

'Polana' SW Late. A short plant with attractive, shiny berries that are susceptible to having a split receptacle, which results in difficulty with fruit removal. Flavor is good, not excellent.

'Polka' NW Midseason. Productive, large, attractive, glossy, medium bright red fruit with good flavor.

'Bristol'/'Munger'

'Navaho'

'Vintage' NW Early. Very productive, with large, very attractive, bright red berries that have outstanding flavor. Can get phytophthora root rot in wet sites.

Black raspberries

'Bristol'/'Munger' NE MW NW SW Early. High-yielding plant with medium-sized, blue-black fruit of excellent flavor and firmness. Needs well-drained soil. Susceptible to anthracnose but tolerant of powdery mildew. There's name confusion: this plant is sold in the East as 'Bristol' and in the West as 'Munger'.

'Jewel' NE MW RM NW Early. Particularly vigorous and productive plant with excellent cold hardiness. Fruit is largest of all available, with fine flavor.

'MacBlack' NW Very late—two weeks after all other cultivars. Vigorous upright plant is productive. Fruit is small to medium, dark, with excellent flavor. The one to plant to extend your season.

Purple raspberries

'Brandywine' NE MW RM NW SW Midseason. Produces firm, round, tart, reddish fruit. Very vigorous, with good cold hardiness.

Suckers grow only from the crown, so plants will not spread.

'Royalty' NE MW RM NW SW Midseason. Soft, cone-shaped fruit that is sweeter than 'Brandywine'. Suckers freely from roots, growing more like a red raspberry in hedgerows. It is resistant to the raspberry aphid but is especially susceptible to crown gall.

Erect blackberries

'Brazos' SE Late. Thorny. Good-sized fruit with large drupelets. Fruit quality is only fair, but the plant is well adapted to regions with low chilling.

'Illini Hardy' NE SE RM Late. Thorny—very. Very hardy. Fair to good fruit quality.

'Kiowa' SE MW Midseason. Thorny. Large flavorful fruit. Plant has a long ripening season and is quite productive.

'Natchez' MW Early to midseason. Thornless. Medium to large fruit is firm and glossy, with good flavor.

'Navaho' NE SE MW NW Mid to late season. Thornless. Small to medium fruit with excellent sweet flavor. Resistant to anthracnose and root rot.

'Chester Thornless'

'Hull Thornless'

'Triple Crown'

'Osage' MW Midseason. Thornless. Productive with medium-sized, good-quality fruit.

'Ouachita' NE SE MW NW Mid to late season. Thornless. Productive, medium-sized fruit with good sweet flavor.

'Prime-Jan' NE SE MW RM Late. Thorny. Plants are very erect, vigorous, and hardy. Fruit is small to medium with moderate firmness. The main reason to plant this one is its cold hardiness.

'Prime-Ark 45' NE SE MW SW Late. Thorny. Firm, medium-sized berries have the best quality of the fall-bearing/primocane-fruiting blackberries. Can ripen too late to get a significant crop.

'Prime-Ark Freedom' MW Late. The first thornless ("freedom from thorns") fall-bearing/primocane-fruiting blackberry. Berries are medium-sized, with moderate firmness and good flavor. Can ripen too late to get a significant crop.

Semi-erect blackberries

'Chester Thornless' NE SE MW NW SW Late. Thornless. Large, deep black, tart berries. Ripens later than 'Hull Thornless' but has better yield and slightly better cold hardiness.

'Doyle's' NE SE MW SW Midseason. Thornless. A newer, widely adaptable variety, touted as super-productive. Disease-resistant. Best trained onto a trellis.

'Hull Thornless' SE MW SW Midseason. Thornless. Flavor is sweeter and less tart than other semi-erect cultivars. Berry does not lose its color in high temperatures.

'Triple Crown' NE SE MW NW SW Late. Thornless. A vigorous plant! Produces very large berries with delicious sweet flavor. Fruit may burn in California's hot-summer areas.

Trailing blackberries

'Black Diamond' SE NW SW Early midseason. Thornless. Moderately vigorous plants form an open canopy, so the fruit is well exposed and thus easy to pick. Productive. Medium to large fruit is conic, uniform, and delicious. A Northwest standard.

'Boysen' SE NW SW Late midseason. Thorny. Vigorous plants produce large crops of large, rough-shaped, maroon-colored berries. Texture is medium to firm. Flavor is outstanding and unique.

'Marion'

'**Columbia Star**' SE NW SW Early to mid-season. Thornless. Vigorous plants produce large crops of big, very uniformly shaped berries with outstanding flavor.

'**Everthornless**' NE SE MW NW SW Late. Thornless. A special selection out of 'Thornless Evergreen' that does not revert to thorny canes. Small, soft, firm berries are dark black and mildly flavored. Derived from the European species *Rubus laciniatus*, so leaves have the cutleaf shape. Plant is very productive.

'**Logan**' SE NW SW Early. Thorny or thornless ('Thornless Logan'). Moderate vigor, moderate crop of raspberry-red, uniformly shaped medium to large berries.

'**Marion**' SE NW SW Midseason. Thorny. The mainstay of the Northwest for 50 years! Typically sold as "marionberry." Plants are vigorous and moderately productive. Medium-sized, aromatic fruit has outstanding flavor; it is, however, soft and a bit irregular.

'**Obsidian**' SE NW SW Very early, among the earliest of all cultivars. Thorny, vigorous plants produce large crops of large, barrel-shaped berries with a strong blackberry flavor. Fruit stays black when refrigerated or frozen.

'**Olallie**' SE NW SW Early. Thorny. Medium to large berries that are bright black and somewhat soft. Plants are vigorous and productive but fairly cold tender. Popular in California.

SITING AND PLANTING

Raspberries, blackberries, and their kin are pretty easy to grow, once you get them started in a suitable location. Of course, to get an optimum harvest, you must plant them right and give them basic care. This includes properly timed tipping and pruning! But the payoff is worth it.

Plants should establish and begin to grow quickly in the first season. Red raspberries begin to fill in the spaces between plants, and black raspberries produce new canes from the crown area. Black raspberry canes tend to grow prostrate, along the ground, in the first year. Stake them up if you can. The next year they will be more upright, and eventually they will be very erect indeed.

First fruit on the fall-bearing blackberries and red and black raspberries will appear in the first year, but the other bramble types will not produce fruit until the following year—remember that all others produce fruit only on two-year-old canes. Even so, your harvest will not be significant for three to four years after planting—but be patient. With luck, you'll have enough fruit in that first or second year to give you the motivation to wait.

The right spot

Choose a spot for your bramble plants out in the open, with ample elbowroom. Because they are not small or naturally tidy plants, site them where those qualities are not going to be a problem. An open, uncluttered part of your yard is also good for other reasons: they'll get the light they need and be exposed to breezes that keep air circulating, thus preventing diseases caused by close quarters or humidity. An open spot surrounded by lawn can be ideal, because you'll be able to see and mow down any suckers that pop up.

Black raspberries should not be planted in soils where potatoes, tomatoes, eggplants, peppers, or strawberries have had a problem with verticillium wilt, since they too are susceptible. Do not plant red raspberry or suckering types of blackberries close to permanent crops in your yard, such as rhubarb or asparagus, because over time their roots may invade.

If the area you've chosen is grassy or full of weeds, after you dig out the spot, you should take the time to improve the soil. Perennial weeds, in particular, will come back to plague you, so kill them before you start. Consider preparing an area a season or more ahead of time. Stake it out, clear it out, then plant a cover crop or green manure crop; this will crowd out weeds and improve the soil's nitrogen levels and—when you cut it down and rototill or dig it in—organic content. Alternatively, solarize the patch's soil, again, a season or more ahead of time.

Light and soil requirements

Brambles require full sun, ideally at least eight hours daily. They can cope with partial shade but will not be as healthy or productive. If there are encroaching trees or other casters of shade nearby, move or remove obstructions, do some significant thinning to let light in—or consider another spot.

Raspberries and blackberries also want well-drained soil. Raspberries do not tolerate wet soils; blackberries are pretty tolerant of wet ground and even short periods of standing water. (If a site is poorly drained, you can plant raspberries in a raised bed that is 6 to 12 inches, 15 to 30 cm higher than the surrounding soil.)

Prior to planting, take the time to increase the organic matter content of the soil. Add well-rotted manure or compost at about 3 pounds (1.5 kg) per 100 square feet (30 m²). This step alone should be sufficient in most cases.

Red raspberries grow best in soil with a pH between 5.0 and 6.0; for blackberries, between 5.0 and 6.5 is fine. Most average soils are in this range, in most areas, but if you have any doubts, get a soil test before planting. Do this up to a year beforehand, so you have time to alter the pH if needed. Apply any necessary lime and phosphorus the fall prior to planting; organic sources include bonemeal and rock phosphate. Potassium can be applied in the fall or spring; organic sources include wood ash and rock potash. Add organic nitrogen sources such as bloodmeal or alfalfa meal in the spring just prior to planting; if you're using regular fertilizer, apply it after planting. After this initial soil adjustment, only nitrogen should be added annually, unless you have reason to suspect some deficiency.

Buying plants

Be sure to obtain your plants from a reputable nursery. Ask around, read online reviews, and study the company's catalog or website to assure yourself that you have chosen wisely. For field-grown plants, it is also a good idea to buy from someone in your same growing region, or similar climate zone; this means the plants will be locally adapted. You want certified virus-free plants.

Tissue-cultured plants are easier to establish and are more likely to be free from disease than dormant canes. They can be planted as soon as the danger of frost has passed. If you acquire dormant canes, plant them in early spring, as soon as the soil can be worked.

If you are planting bare-root plants, unwrap and examine your starts as soon as you get them home. Trim off damaged or limp growth. Store them in a cool, shady place where they won't dry out (wrap them in damp newspaper, if needed) until you are ready to plant; you can hold them for up to a week, if necessary. Tissue-cultured plug plants should be kept watered and in the sun but protected from frosts on cold nights, until planting.

Planting day

Choose a cloudy or drizzly day in early spring to plant, to minimize stress on the young plants. If planting bare-root plants, be sure to soak the roots in water thoroughly (several hours in a bucket) prior to planting. Then, as you work, take care that the roots don't dry out. Remove them one at a time from the water bucket or cover the bare roots with a damp towel. For plugs, make sure they do not dry out during the planting day, but do not leave them in standing water either. Treat them as you would a vegetable transplant.

Dig a deep planting hole and, if your soil lacks fertility, or is particularly heavy (full of clay) or light (sandy), replace about half the soil with well-aged compost. Set plants at just slightly deeper than they were in

RESTRAINING RED RASPBERRIES

Red raspberry plants make a wonderful hedge. But their suckering nature has the potential to create tensions with neighbors, of both the human and plant variety. Be sure to isolate their root systems at planting time. Use a plastic underground barrier, at least 12 inches (30 cm) deep. Otherwise the raspberry plants will overtake ornamentals in the vicinity (although peonies are worthy opponents).

the nursery, but be careful—don't bury or smother them, either. Bring along the hose or watering can and soak the hole before planting.

Young plants have shallow root systems, so it is important to water them in very well immediately after planting. You should also mulch between the plants and between the rows—read on for details.

Planting plans

Whether you put in a short or long row, or have the space and ambition for a few rows, there is more to do to assure success than appropriate spacing. You should also have a system in mind. Here's the scoop.

Spacing between plants. Plants should be spaced within rows as follows: red raspberries, 24 to 36 inches (60 to 90 cm); black and purple raspberries, 36 inches (90 cm); erect blackberries, 40 to 48 inches (100 to 120 cm); and semi-erect and trailing blackberries, 4 to 6 feet (1.2 to 1.8 m) apart.

Spacing between rows. Rows should be at least 10 feet (3 m) apart. If this sounds excessive, just wait—you'll see the sense in it. Row spacing depends on the size of the equipment that will be used to maintain (mow) the planting; at least 4 feet (1.2 m)

more than the widest implement should be left between rows if more than one row is planted. Even if you are cultivating by hand, be sure to leave plenty of room to move freely between the rows.

Hedgerows. This is less work but often less satisfactory. Used with raspberries and some blackberries. Most raspberries can get by with such passive support, thanks to their relatively stiff canes—but this is not optimum. Still, if you are a casual gardener or are letting the raspberries double as a physical barrier or living fence on a property line, you could try it. The key is to plant them even more closely than recommended and let them lean on each other for support—which they will do, in time. The drawbacks are that a dense planting is harder to harvest from, and diseases and other pests can gain a foothold in a row with limited air flow.

Trellis systems. All blackberry and raspberry types require support. It may be as simple as some posts and bailing twine for fall-bearing raspberries or a full-blown trellis for the more vigorous blackberries. The value of providing support for raspberry plants in particular is nothing new: "The cost of stakes is but a trifle in comparison to the value of the fruit lost when they are

It is possible to grow raspberries in hedgerows, as large, rambling bushes.

You will find that raspberry plants are a lot easier to manage and harvest from if you provide a trellis. The stems have no natural way to hold on, such as tendrils, so you must tie them on as they grow.

BRAMBLE SUPPORTS.

There are various ways to support your erect-growing bramble plants.

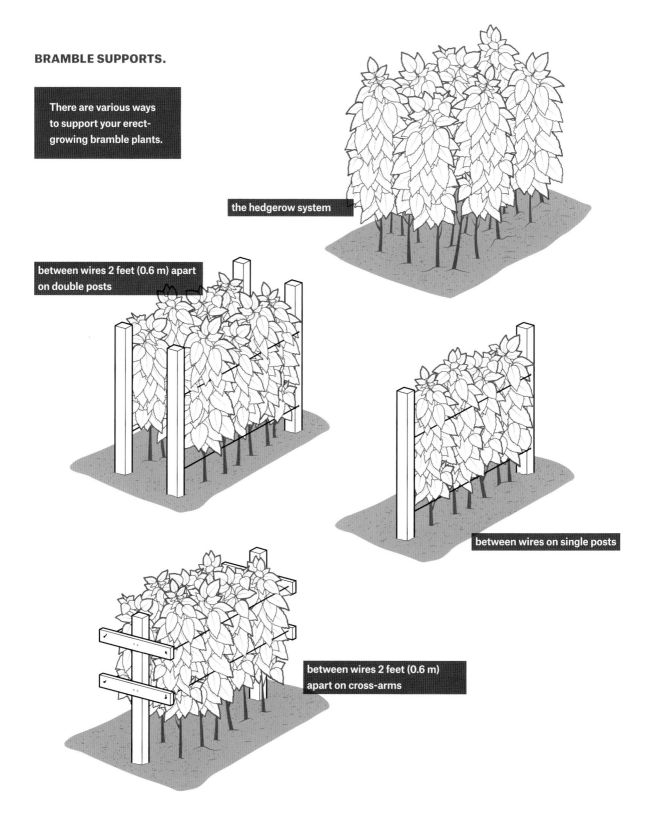

the hedgerow system

between wires 2 feet (0.6 m) apart on double posts

between wires on single posts

between wires 2 feet (0.6 m) apart on cross-arms

Put in strong, sturdy posts at each end of a bramble planting; be sure to sink them deeply into the ground so mature plants can't pull them down or make them lean. Run wire or strong twine between them to help control and guide the plants.

not used" (Andrew S. Fuller, *The Small Fruit Culturist*, 1881).

The advantages of trellising go beyond merely supporting floppy or bushy plants. They will be better restrained. Picking will be easier. You'll be able to keep track of where the planting begins and ends. Trellis systems generally do not affect the type of pruning a plant receives. Rather, the trellis allows the plant to support more surface area for fruit production, that is, a larger canopy—obviously, a big plus.

You'd be wise to have on hand and install your trellis system on planting day or very soon afterward. This is not a project to undertake when the plants are lustily

A more extensive blackberry planting calls for ample support in the form of a sturdy "T" system.

growing! Vertical posts can be wooden or metal, and in most cases are best at 5 to 6 feet (1.5 to 1.8 m) tall. The horizontal "guides" can be heavy-gauge galvanized wire, or strong nylon twine or rope (though these latter two, of course, slacken and wear down over time and need to be replaced). Sink posts deeply so they won't wobble or lean (thus, their initial height should be about 8 feet, 2.5 m). Fasten the guides by whatever means is secure, strong, and works for you (tying, bolts, nails, eye hooks). Placing guides 2 to 3 feet (0.6 to 1 m) apart is sufficient for most bramble plants, but you can fine-tune this as you become more experienced.

THE TIES THAT BIND

Whether you intend to fasten canes to a trellis, or wires or rope, or even a fence, here's how to do it so the canes stay or grow where you want:

- Intervene earlier rather than later. New green growth is more flexible.

- Be gentle. Do not tug or yank, or you may bend or snap off canes or dislodge shallow roots.

- Tie lower down first and work your way up the canes, vertically, before moving on to horizontal training.

- Use surveyor's tape, rags, torn-up lengths from old T-shirts, old pantyhose, or other soft and somewhat flexible material in preference to wire, rubber bands, twine, or string.

- Make an ample loop around the cane first, then tie the ends to the support. This allows movement but prevents laceration when the wind blows the plant around, say, during a summer thunderstorm.

Horizontal or "T" system. Tall posts, each with at least one horizontal cross-arm, support wires or rope running down each side of a planting. For summer-bearing raspberries and blackberries, this system will support canes until they fruit. A disadvantage is that you have to guess how tall the plants will get when you install the cross-arm; a way around this is to install multiple cross-arms at various heights. For fall-bearing raspberries and erect blackberries, this system will hold up the canes for the six or so weeks that the plants are fruiting; you can detach the wires or rope later when you need to mow the canes to the ground.

CARING FOR YOUR PLANTS

Mulching

Weed control in the first year is essential. After planting, apply a deep mulch. Use 4 inches (10 cm) of clean straw; *do not* use hay, which harbors weed seeds. Some gardeners swear by bark mulch (fir, pine, whatever), small chunks or slabs of a rock mulch, or a combination of the two. Be careful on red raspberries in wet climates as you may cause the root system to remain wet during winter, leading to root rot.

For red raspberries and erect blackberries, which send suckers up from the roots,

You should apply a good mulch right after planting to keep weeds at bay while the bramble plants get established. Leave it in place, allowing it to break down. Do not refresh it later that season or in subsequent years; too much mulch may encourage soil-borne fungal diseases.

be sure to also mulch between the rows. Alternatively, allowing or establishing a sod cover between the rows is a good idea.

Important: *do not* mulch the following year and beyond (unless your soil is very sandy)! Mulch, especially on heavy or clayey soils, is known to encourage the development of soil-borne fungal diseases that weaken and eventually kill some bramble plants.

Watering

Steady, sufficient moisture is really important for a good berry crop. Raspberries and blackberries generally require about 2 inches (5 cm) of water per week during the growing season, and 2 to 4 inches (5 to 10 cm) per week when the berries are developing.

Drip or trickle irrigation or soaker hoses are preferable to overhead sprinkling because wetting the fruit increases the risk of disease. Irrigation experiments have shown that the response of the raspberry plant is very linear—that is, the more water you give it, the taller it gets. Up to a point, this is a good thing, but you do not want your plants to get so tall that they cannot support the fruit they are bearing. This is usually only a problem with the fall-bearing red raspberries.

Fertilizing

If the soil was properly prepared (and possibly adjusted) prior to planting to meet the nutrient requirements of your plants, only nitrogen will need to be added going forward.

Here are the standard recommendations, which you can adjust according to your site's soil and the performance of your plants as the years go by. Apply a half-pound (0.25 kg) of actual nitrogen per 100 feet (30 m) of row once the soil has settled around the roots well. In subsequent years, you can increase the nitrogen levels to as high as 1 pound (0.5 kg) of actual nitrogen per 100 feet (30 m) of row, applied in the late spring (approximately April or May). Feed any fall-bearing cultivars an additional 0.2 to 0.3 pound of nitrogen (per 100 feet, 30 m) in late June or early July. If you don't use commercial fertilizer, organic nitrogen sources include bloodmeal and alfalfa meal.

If you did not test your soil prior to planting, play it safe. Side-dress each spring with good rotted manure or compost, or apply a balanced 10-10-10 fertilizer.

PRUNING

If you want to enjoy good berry harvests, pruning is not optional. Not with brambles. Don't delay for a few years, or get complacent and neglect your bushes. Prune *every* year.

Prune to thin, that is, to reduce crowding and allow air in—not to mention your own hands in search of those delicious fruits. Prune also to help the plants through their life cycle. It turns out that fruiting canes of all cultivated raspberries and blackberries, with the exception of the fall-bearing types, die after fruiting is completed. These dead floricanes should be removed immediately after fruiting—they're never going to come back to life. Taking them out also improves air circulation through the canopy and helps keep the planting as tidy as possible ("under control" might be an overstatement!). Here

are some recommendations for specific pruning situations.

Pruning summer-bearing red raspberries

Summer-bearing red raspberries will grow naturally in a hedgerow system. The new shoots, originating from the root system, will fill in the entire length of the row. No summer pruning (except for removing spent floricanes) is necessary, although suckers growing outside the desired area may be removed at any time. In fact, if your raspberries are growing in a good location, they'll probably attempt a mutiny and try to take over your yard and the rest of the universe. Mowing the canes back when they are small is usually sufficient to keep them in check.

Dormant pruning for summer-bearing red raspberries can be accomplished any time the canes are fully dormant (November through March in northern regions). At that time, remove all dead, damaged, or weak canes, and try to narrow the beds to 12 to 18 inches (30 to 45 cm). This last is a very important step. If the beds get too wide, light (which fuels flower bud development) cannot penetrate well, and the canopy gets so dense that it does not dry quickly, which promotes fungal diseases. Further, the rows become difficult to work in, and fruit within the canopy is often not seen, left to rot, and disseminates disease-causing spores.

Raspberry bushes are not only lusty growers, they sucker a lot.

After narrowing the beds, thin the canes so that there is about one cane every 4 to 6 inches (10 to 15 cm) within the row. Try to leave the healthiest canes with the largest cane diameter. The canes you leave standing should look sturdy. Imagine hanging a crop of fruit on them: will they stay upright or topple over?

Pruning fall-bearing red raspberries

Fall-bearing red raspberries bear fruit on canes produced in the first season (hence their alternative name: primocane-fruiting red raspberries). In late summer, the canes stop growing and develop flower buds. Flowering and fruit development begins at the tip of the cane and continues successively down the cane toward the base. When the weather becomes cold enough, flowering and fruiting cease.

To dormant-prune fall-bearing raspberries, simply remove all the canes at the base, as close to the ground as possible, and begin the cycle again the next spring. Alternatively, canes that fruited in the fall can be left in place and allowed to fruit the following summer. Unpruned canes on this type of raspberry begin flowering at the node below the last fruit of the previous year, and they will bear fruit in early to midsummer.

You can leave the canes over the winter and get a smaller crop from them the following season, or you can mow the canes off and just gather the fall crop. It's up to you whether you want to sacrifice that early-summer treat for a smaller but arguably better-tasting late crop.

Pruning black and purple raspberries

Unlike red raspberries, black and purple raspberries, in addition to removal of spent floricanes, require summer tipping (removing their tips) at 3 to 4 feet (1 to 1.2 m) if they are not grown on a trellis. Tipping encourages the development of lateral fruiting branches and increases the strength of the cane. Do this fairly early in the season, at which point only 3 to 6 inches (7.5 to 15 cm) of new growth needs to be removed. In the eastern United States, tipping the plants later than this—when removal of more than 6 inches (15 cm) of new growth is required to bring the height back to 4 feet (1.2 m)—can increase the incidence of cane blight (see page 120), since the resulting wound, from removing wood that is larger in diameter, takes longer to heal. This is not a problem in the Pacific Northwest.

All dead, damaged, and weak canes should be removed from dormant black and purple raspberry plants. Thin the remaining canes to five to ten per plant. Head back lateral branches to around 4 to 6 inches (10 to 15 cm) for black raspberries, or 6 to 10 inches (15 to 25 cm) for the purple ones. More vigorous plants can support longer lateral branches. If any sort of trellis system is used,

canes can be tipped higher (up to 5 feet, 1.5 m) as long as the trellis supports them.

Pruning erect blackberries

Erect blackberries have strong upright canes. They should be pruned similarly to black and purple raspberries: tipped back to 3 to 4 feet (1 to 1.2 m) in the summer, with laterals cut back to 12 to 18 inches (30 to 45 cm) in the dormant season. Because they produce new shoots from the root system, erect blackberries may be grown in hedgerows. If you do this, dormant-prune to thin the canes to about 10 inches (25 cm) apart.

Pruning semi-erect blackberries

Semi-erect blackberries are not naturally upright in habit and thus require trellising. A simple trellis with wires at heights of 3 and 6 feet (1 and 1.8 m) is the most common approach, although the plants also can be trained to fences or other structures up to 8 feet (2.5 m) in height. Plant height will depend on soil fertility and water availability.

Tip the semi-erect plants to about 5 feet (1.5 m) and tie the lateral branches during the summer months. For dormant pruning, retain about five to eight of the strongest canes, and remove laterals that originate on the lower 3 feet (1 m) of the main canes. Shorten the remaining laterals to 12 to 18 inches (30 to 45 cm).

Fortunately, this is not a big task.

Relatively few canes are produced per plant, and a little careful training of the canes as they grow takes a small amount of time, though a great amount of *timing*. Be sure to train the canes while they are still green. They have a tendency to break off at the base if bent too far, so tie them vertically first, and then train the tips of the shoots horizontally, if desired.

Pruning trailing blackberries

Trailing blackberry primocanes trail along the ground for many feet and must be lifted up and tied to a trellis. The primocanes are not tipped, as they are in the other blackberry types. As with the semi-erect blackberries, a substantial trellis with wires at heights of 3 and 6 feet (1 and 1.8 m) is the most common approach.

Canes can either be lifted in the late summer or left on the ground over the winter. If plants are fall-trained, yields will be higher, but there is greater risk of winter injury. Spring-trained plants, on the other hand, will have lower yields. They'll have less winter injury but are tricky to train, as the canes can be fairly brittle in the spring. Whenever training is done, thin to six to 10 canes and remove any weak ones.

Revitalizing old brambles

Perhaps you inherited a patch of bramble bushes from the last person to garden on your property, or the person before that. It's become a big, impenetrable, prickly tangle. But you've glimpsed a few pretty berries in there, and you'd like to bring back the plant or plants. If it's a cultivar, not a rangy, disease-ridden wildling, it may be worth your effort.

A neglected caneberry will require determined and brave work, but it can be done. Tackle the plant in early spring, while it is still dormant, before it leafs out, so it can recover from your cuts heading into the new growing season.

The first step is protecting yourself if you face thorny types: step out to this job in heavy clothing, heavy boots, a good-fitting hat, and tough gloves. Bring along sharp tools: loppers and clippers, and maybe a small handsaw as well. Also bring along a bin, wheelbarrow, or tarp upon which to put the prunings so they will be easier to cart away.

Survey the general area and start by cutting down all wandering suckers, so that you can work with the actual mother plant. Once close to that, remove at ground level all obviously dead, diseased, and/or damaged canes. Next, take out any young canes that are crowded or spindly. Stand back and assess what's left. If there's still a lot of plant, go back in and thin to eight to 10 good, young canes.

If you are lucky, the previous gardener supplied supports that are now revealed by

You can bring back caneberries that have been neglected. Some judicious pruning, some weed-pulling, some training (including perhaps discovering and, if necessary, repairing or replacing supports), and you're back in business.

your foray into the overgrown plant. Fix them back up or install new ones, including new wires, because you will want to support this season's new canes for eventual harvest.

One last note: if you're dealing with a big and old planting, you might not be able to tell right away what was an original plant, or make out rows. In such a case, head in there with the plan of creating a wide alley—8 to 10 feet (2.5 to 3 m) would be good—between the revived rows of plants. Otherwise, you may still not be able to reach the fruit once the canes have leafed out and produced laterals.

HARVESTING AND AFTERCARE

So you've chosen the berry you wanted (a good cultivar for your area), planted carefully, tended, trellised, tipped, and tied—of course you are eager to taste the fruits of your labors! The following is basic information on how to harvest and how to care for your plants in the off-season, so you'll keep reaping those rewards in coming years.

Picking

At last, the moment has arrived! At least, you think so. Here's how to tell. Ripe

Determining the ripeness of the berries takes some practice.

raspberries detach easily from their receptacle or core. Blackberries, by contrast, do not separate from their core; you'll have to pluck them off and go by fruit color and flavor. After they've colored up, sample a few, some each day, until a berry "hits the sweet spot," and you stand there among your big thorny bushes exclaiming, "Ah! *That's it!*"

On harvesting day, you ought to wear gloves or at least long sleeves to minimize scratches and pokes from the prickles and thorns. Like all small-fruit crops, raspberries and blackberries are best harvested in the morning, after the dew has dried; harvesting berries during the coolest part of the morning leads to longer shelf life.

Bring out a number of small containers rather than one big one. And spare yourself a moment of congratulations for choosing to grow caneberries, because at harvesting time, the labor is not backbreaking. Unlike strawberries, you don't have to bend over the whole time, or sit down and scoot along the ground. Your quarry is mainly at eye and hand level.

Berries should be stacked no more than three or four high in shallow containers; stacking them higher crushes the berries on the bottom. In the thick of the harvest season, try putting "extra" berries directly onto a baking sheet and freezing—for about a day—as you go. (Once they're frozen, transfer them to storage containers or airtight baggies; they'll keep six to eight months.)

Raspberries are notorious for their short shelf life. This is due, in part, to the morphology of the fruit, which is composed of many loosely attached drupelets. It is also a result of the fruit's high rate of respiration (basically, they "sweat" juice) after harvest, which is the highest of any temperate-zone fruit.

How can you maximize berry shelf life? Work quickly when picking, and if the harvest is big, pause and take frequent trips into the house to get them out of the sun. Keep them out of direct sunlight in any event. Do not wash the fruit until you are ready to use it, as this decreases quality and leads to rot problems (when you do wash berries, handle them very gently—shaking in a colander over the sink might bruise them).

Put all berries in the refrigerator as soon as possible: cold temperatures are the best preservative. Try blotting wet ones with absorbent paper towels, putting them into a salad spinner, or even arraying them in a single layer on plates or cookie sheets and running a fan in their direction for a bit. Freeze raspberries as soon as possible. Blackberries can be handled similarly, although their shelf life is several days longer than that of raspberries.

Overwintering

As winter approaches, bramble bushes don't need any special care in most areas. Just like the rest of your garden plants, they should be tidied up and the area around them cleared of debris (leaves, twigs, fallen fruit). Spent fruiting canes (floricanes), damaged, and dead or diseased ones should be cut

out, if you haven't done this already. There is no need to mulch the roots for the winter beyond what you already have in place, assuming you've chosen a cultivar that is suitable for your area.

Trailing blackberries are an exception. If you are growing these in an area with very cold winters, you'd be wise to leave the primocanes on the ground and mulch them over. When spring returns, you can resurrect them; wait as long as possible, because the canes can snap if they are still fairly cold. Remove the mulch and train them up on the wire system you installed previously; now floricanes, they are ready for the next season.

TROUBLESHOOTING

When it comes to pest prevention and control for your brambles, as with all edible plants, you'll want to avoid chemical sprays. The good news is, most problems in a home berry patch can be prevented, thwarted, or at least managed without ever resorting to spraying anything.

Fungal diseases

These can be the bane of caneberry growers, particularly in wet and humid areas. Commercial growers often resort to fungicides, but you needn't—not with your much smaller patch. Many of the following cane disease problems are better solved in the backyard

Although it usually appears on blackberries and raspberries postharvest, gray mold can (rarely) appear in the garden. Either way, it's ugly and renders the fruits inedible.

Spots on the leaves of your bramble bushes usually indicate a fungal disease. Shown here is a raspberry plant afflicted with anthracnose.

with dormant winter applications of lime sulfur (which is, granted, smelly). Lime sulfur occurs naturally and is approved for use by organic growers.

Cane blight (pathogen: *Leptosphaeria coniothyrium*) is a destructive disease that is most often a problem on black raspberries, although it does occasionally occur on red and purple raspberries, and sometimes on blackberries. Cane blight is generally most problematic during particularly wet years on wounded or damaged canes. Affected primocanes develop dark red to purple lesions; badly infected ones die back, turning silver to gray as they decline. Make sure to prune out and destroy (burn, send away with the

trash) any diseased canes before new canes develop in the spring. Also, avoid pinching primocanes during periods of wet weather to avoid infection.

Gray mold (pathogen: *Botrytis cinerea*) afflicts caneberries as well as strawberries. The important practical difference though is that, unlike with strawberries, gray mold almost never develops on raspberries or blackberries that are still attached to the plant, unless the fruit is overripe or it is an exceptionally rainy year. If you keep your fruit well harvested, refrigerate or freeze it as soon as you pick it, and consume it promptly, you can pretty much avoid gray mold. However, gray mold can form on fruit in the refrigerator. It develops on blackberries and raspberries in the refrigerator much more rapidly than it does with strawberries, so be aware of the possibility—and eat your berries quickly.

Anthracnose (pathogen: *Elsinoë veneta*) is occasionally a problem on these plants. Symptoms are spots on leaves and lesions on canes, particularly of black raspberries; individual drupelets can also look "scabby" in wet years. A dormant liquid lime-sulfur spray—which stinks, is caustic, and is a pain to use but is organic and sometimes necessary—can be applied just as the plants are starting to grow, when leaves are expanded to about ½ inch (1 cm). If the plants have been sited and pruned properly, however, spraying will rarely be necessary.

Phytophthora root rot (pathogen: *Phytophthora fragariae* var. *rubi*) generally affects only red raspberries, but you may encounter it on other brambles, especially on marginal, poorly drained sites and in particularly wet years. Plants collapse early in the summer, when the water demands of the foliage and fruit exceed what the dead or dying roots can provide. In summer-bearing types, it can also result in high plant mortality after the winter. If your site is marginally wet, planting in raised beds will help enormously to reduce the incidence of this disease; plant atop mounds or berms that are 12 to 18 inches (30 to 45 cm) tall. You may need to routinely mound up more soil if the raspberry roots become exposed.

Viral diseases

Just as viruses cannot be controlled but only outlived by humans, they also cannot be controlled in plants. In other words, once a plant has a virus, its presence is permanent. Infected plants exhibit disease symptoms each year, whereas other sorts of disease may come and go. That said, raspberries and blackberries can host many viruses with few symptoms. A few are debilitating, leading to berries that are so crumbly, they can't be harvested, or weak plants that are more susceptible to winter damage. Some can outright kill your plants.

How do you know if your plants have a virus? Diagnosis is not easy. Often plants will simply be stunted and not grow well. A virus found in red raspberries makes the fruit crumbly, causing the drupelets to fall apart when you pick a berry. Mosaic virus, a problem in black raspberries, can cause a mosaic-like pattern to develop on the lower leaves in the spring, but this is an easy symptom to miss. You could send samples to a virus-testing laboratory to confirm whether the leaves are infected.

The bottom line is that, at all costs, you want to avoid viruses. Here are some steps you can take:

1. Purchase plants from a reputable nursery that advertises its plants as virus-tested. Despite the convenience (and price tag), digging up plants from a neighbor's garden carries too many risks.
2. Remove wild brambles growing in the vicinity of your cultivated raspberries or blackberries, if practical. They are reservoirs not only for viruses but also for orange rust, a systemic fungal disease that sometimes infects erect and semi-erect blackberries in the eastern United States.
3. Control the vectors (carriers) of viruses, if you can.

The primary vectors for viruses are aphids and nematodes. You can have your soil tested for nematodes, but unless the soil is very sandy or your area has a history of nematodes, it is probably not necessary to do so. One of the most common virus problems in red raspberry, raspberry bushy dwarf virus, is symptomless other than crumbly fruit. Unfortunately for gardeners and farmers, this one is pollen-borne and the vector is bees—no way to control that!

Common pests and other problems

Weeds need to be controlled vigilantly in new plantings, but once established, raspberries and blackberries are excellent competitors; few weeds will succeed in their presence. Sap beetles and tarnished plant bug can plague brambles as they can strawberries (see that chapter for more details), but they usually are not much of a problem. Indeed, raspberries and blackberries, if planted in a good site, are relatively devoid of insect and other pest problems, with a few notable exceptions.

Japanese beetles. In areas of the United States and Canada where Japanese beetles are prevalent, you can expect to see these pests annually on your raspberry or blackberry plants. If numbers are low, as they tend to be in cooler years, you can just ignore them or simply knock them off the plants into a bucket of soapy water. In most years, however, when numbers are high, they can do quite a bit of damage to the leaves. (Remember that leaves are providing fuel for the entire plant system.) Fortunately, timing is in the gardener's favor here: Japanese beetles usually create the biggest problem after summer-bearing fruit is harvested and well before fall-bearing types begin fruiting.

Pheromone traps are a much-advertised means of controlling Japanese beetles without the use of pesticides. These traps are plastic bags that contain the mating scent of the beetle. In a good Japanese beetle year (which is, by definition, a tough raspberry year), these bags will quickly fill with beetles, requiring emptying at least once a day. The problem is that these bags are probably bringing in all the neighborhood beetles, and

you may not be making much of a dent in the overall population.

Another remedy is the use of milky spore, which is a bacterium that infects the Japanese beetle grubs when they are still in the ground. It is usually sold as a powder that you can spread on any turf area, where the grubs overwinter, during the dormant season (fall through spring). A couple of caveats: milky spore works only in warmer climates, specifically zones 6 to 10, and all the lawn in the vicinity needs to be treated in order for the control to be effective. In other words, there's no point in treating your own yard if the guy behind you doesn't treat his because the Japanese beetles won't pay any attention to the fence.

Spotted wing drosophila (*Drosophila suzukii*) is a type of vinegar fly. The males are easily identified due to two spots on their little wings. This relatively new threat, originally from Japan, emerged as a problem on the West Coast in 2008 and is now found throughout all but the coldest berry production areas of the United States and Canada. Red raspberries and blackberries are among its favorite targets. It goes after healthy berries (rather than overripe or damaged fruit, as fruit flies would). Affected fruit literally melts down, and mold soon moves in. Keep a lookout and take preventive measures: keep your fruit picked, and remove and get rid of old and affected fruit.

Birds. Raspberries and blackberries are not nearly as popular as blueberries with these notorious pests of berry plants. In some areas, though, birds relish black raspberries—the first to ripen. The culprits may be robins, catbirds, and brown thrashers, to name a few. The remedy? You can try traditional scare tactics, from flapping pie tins and flash/shimmer tape to a fierce-looking plastic owl or a blasting radio. But by far the best deterrent is good bird netting (get it at any garden or home supply store). Remember to anchor it down. If you have a larger planting, you'd do well to install overhead support, upon which to drape the netting.

Intense sunlight and heat. Intense sunlight caused by ultraviolet (UV) radiation, with or without accompanying heat, can cause real problems with brambles. In blackberries, the symptoms are either a checkered pattern of white or red drupelets (most commonly seen in the erect blackberries) or the sunny side of the fruit turning pink and mushy (more common in trailing and semi-erect blackberries). In raspberries, the symptoms are a checkered pattern of white drupelets, an entire section of white drupelets, or the sunny side of the fruit becoming pink and mushy.

RASPBERRIES AND BLACKBERRIES are not tricky to grow. Harvests can be downright bountiful—weigh that against the expense when these berries are purchased! And their flavor—when "you pick" berries at the peak of ripeness on a bright morning and eat them fresh (and "free")—is indescribably vibrant. Neither overly sugary nor too tart, each berry delivers a little explosion of succulent sweetness. Once you've tasted success with a mainstream raspberry or blackberry patch, make it a point to seek out and grow some of the less common types: a ripe yellow raspberry or plump, juicy loganberry is an epic treat well within reach of a home gardener.

blueberries

BLUEBERRIES: HOW CAN YOU GO WRONG?

Sometimes the reward of growing your own blueberries is measured in terms of immediate satisfaction, like a handful scattered on a bowl of granola or into the blender for your morning smoothie. Other times, the gratification is delayed but just as sweet (homemade blueberry preserves spiced with touches of cinnamon and nutmeg, or a freezer bag of pie-worthy berries in the middle of winter). And the plants themselves are exceedingly ornamental, bringing excitement and color to the landscape throughout the seasons.

Even if you have room for only one blueberry plant, go for it—not only can you look forward to a tasty harvest, but the easy-care bush will contribute its tidy form and seasonal color shows to your garden for years to come.

In spring, there are clusters of delicate, bell-shaped blossoms, white to pink in color. Once pollinated, those flowers give rise to our luscious blueberries. Come fall, the lovely bright green, sometimes glossy leaves flame a fiery red. And the twigs of most cultivars also turn red—a wonderful contrast in the winter garden to the muted colors of most vegetation or to the latest blanket of white snow.

Blueberries have been grown in cultivated plantations since the early 1900s, but low-bush blueberries in New England and the Canadian Maritimes, like the huckleberry fields of the Pacific Northwest, were managed long before that. Native peoples used fire to rejuvenate the plants and eliminate weeds, much as commercial growers still do. The fact that blueberries are native to North America is significant to backyard growers

Beautiful and good for you, too: blueberries make even the shortest superfood list.

BENEFICIAL BLUEBERRIES

Blueberries have enjoyed a surge in popularity recently because of more thorough knowledge of their health benefits. They are naturally very high in antioxidants; these are thought to help neutralize free radicals in the human body, which have been implicated in various diseases including cancer. Antioxidants are also useful in combatting intestinal bacteria. Indeed, blueberries have more antioxidants than many other fruits and vegetables—double that of spinach, and three times as much as fresh oranges.

Fans of jams and jellies may already know that blueberries are high in pectin. Pectin is found in other fruits, of course, notably apples, but blueberries—fresh or processed with their skins on—are a good source of this soluble fiber. A diet high in fiber is good for you in many ways, including the facts that it aids digestion and lowers cholesterol.

in the United States and Canada. For one thing, because the plant evolved here, it co-evolved with numerous pests. Bad news, right? No, good news, because the plants also evolved mechanisms for pest resistance. When planted in a suitable spot, blueberry bushes tend to be blessedly pest-free.

The form of blueberry plants varies, from the lowbush blueberry (*Vaccinium angustifolium*), which makes an effective groundcover and propagates by underground stolons, to the northern highbush blueberry (*V. corymbosum*), which often reaches 10 feet (3 m) in height in its natural habitat, to the rabbiteye blueberry (*V. virgatum*), which can attain a height of 20 feet (6 m) in southern locations. Most of the information that follows pertains

to the northern highbush blueberry, the main type available to home gardeners, although the other types are discussed as well.

The northern highbush blueberry is indigenous to North America, and native peoples have long treasured its berries, fresh and dried. Interest in growing the crop on a commercial scale first emerged in the mid-1800s. Selection and breeding research was initiated shortly after the turn of the century by Elizabeth White, a cranberry producer in Whitesbog, New Jersey. White used "monetary incentives" to obtain the largest fruited blueberry plants flourishing in the Pine Barrens of New Jersey. The story goes—perhaps apocryphal—that she asked natives of the barrens to bring her large fruit, and if the fruit failed to pass through her wedding band, she acquired the bush from which the berries came (berries over 16 mm ended up being favored). White then transplanted these bushes to a site for observation. Frederick Coville, a plant breeder at the USDA in Beltsville, Maryland, became interested in the crop and, in 1906, began the first blueberry breeding program with material White had selected from the wild. One of those original wild selections, 'Rubel', is grown to this day. But the blueberry's value as a fruit crop was not truly exploited until the 1920s, perhaps because it was so easy to harvest in the wild that it was unnecessary to cultivate it.

Selection work with wild blueberries has led to a bounty of garden-worthy cultivars that are both productive and good-looking. Just be sure you like the flavor of the one or ones you choose. Larger berries do not always mean sweeter fruit; in fact, some of the bigger-fruited "improvements" have less flavor. This is because flavor resides in the skins, not the flesh inside. Thus a pie made of small blueberries has more skin than a pie made of large ones, and therefore more intense flavor!

ABOUT THE PLANT

The blueberry is different in that it prefers soil in which most of our other berry plants would not thrive or even grow. Blueberry plants grow best in soils that are acidic (pH 4.5 to 5.0), uniformly moist (not wet), and nutrient-poor. Why? The species evolved in swamps, wetlands, and pond- and streamsides. Thus, blueberries generally tolerate fluctuating soil water conditions better than other plants.

Blueberry root systems are fibrous but lack root hairs, though this does not appear to have a negative impact on their ability to get the plant the water and nutrients it needs. It turns out that blueberry plants have a fungus living in their root systems that helps them acquire nutrients from tough soils. The fungus and the blueberry plant have a symbiotic relationship—that is, the two organisms cooperate with and benefit from each other: the fungus provides nutrients for the plant, and the plant provides the fungus with food (carbohydrates from photosynthesis). This cooperation between the fungus and the roots is a mycorrhizal association (from the Latin, *myco* = "fungus," *rhiza* = "root").

Fruit size in blueberries is determined by several factors. Firstly, genetics: wild blueberry plants produce fruit that is generally much smaller than the cultivated blueberry fruit we see in our grocery stores and at fruit stands. (Certainly, anyone who has ever picked less-than-pea-sized wild blueberries has marveled, nay, despaired, at how long it takes to fill a bucket, or even a pint, with these small packets of aromatic flavor.)

A blueberry bush in full bloom. Blueberries are best pollinated by native bumblebees, which evolved alongside the urn-shaped flowers.

In addition to genetic makeup, berry size is affected by the amount of nutrients and water available when flower buds are initiated in late summer and when the fruit develops the following summer. Insufficient water during fruit sizing, in particular, leads to smaller berries. Keep in mind, however, that too much water just before harvest can lead to bland-flavored, if large, fruit.

Pollination can also influence fruit size: the fruit will be noticeably larger if the flowers are cross-pollinated (pollinated with pollen from a different cultivar) rather than self-pollinated. Native bumblebees are the best pollinators for blueberries since they pollinate over a wide range of weather conditions and are extremely active. They tend to do a better job than honeybees, which are not native to North America.

Cool temperatures (below 50°F, 10°C) restrict pollination in two ways. The bees do not fly as much when the weather is cool or rainy. Too, even if the pollen has landed on the stigma (in other words, the flower is pollinated), it still needs to germinate, grow a tube down the stigma, and fertilize the waiting egg. If the weather is cool, this process is slowed down considerably.

Finally, unpruned blueberries with lots of old wood and many flower buds will produce smaller fruit than well-pruned blueberries. Studies have shown that blueberries from properly pruned bushes can be 10 to 15 percent larger than those from unpruned bushes of the same variety in the same field—something for the home gardener to bear in mind.

BLUEBERRY TYPES

Northern highbush blueberry

Northern highbush blueberry (*Vaccinium corymbosum*; zones 3 to 7) is the primary type available to home gardeners. It has a relatively shallow root system and woody canes that originate from its crown. A mature cultivated specimen commonly has 15 to 18 shoots, or canes. Growth habit varies among cultivars; some form very upright bushes, others are more spreading in habit. Depending on the cultivar, expect to pick from mid to late summer. These plants need cooler winters in order to thrive and set fruit. Southern Canada and many parts of the United States are suitable for growing this type.

Southern highbush blueberry

Southern highbush blueberries (zones [5]6 to 10) are a cross between *Vaccinium corymbosum* and various species native to the South, including *V. darrowii*, a southern native with a spicy, fragrant taste. The resulting hybrids, bred for their low chilling requirement and good fruit flavor, can grow in climates with mild winters. (The chilling requirement is a mechanism whereby plants need a certain number of hours between 35 and 45°F before they will break bud and flower.)

Thanks to these hybrids, blueberry growing has expanded further south, to California, to Mexico, throughout a large part of South America, and into southern Europe and Africa. Southern highbush blueberries don't do well in the North, as they either die from midwinter cold or, when there is a midwinter warm spell, they begin to flower because their chilling requirement has been met.

Lowbush blueberry

The lowbush blueberry (*Vaccinium angustifolium*; zones [2]3 to 6) is a low, sprawling shrub. It holds promise for the backyard grower interested in cultivating an edible groundcover no more than 15 to 24 inches (40 to 60 cm) high. Unfortunately, very few cultivars are available to home gardeners, primarily from New England specialty

TYPICAL BLUEBERRY HARVEST TIMES

California	March–June
Northeast	late July–September
Southeast	April–May
Midwest	mid-July–early September
Rocky Mountain	mid-July–early September
Northwest	July–September
Southwest	April–June

nurseries that carry novelty fruits. Lowbush blueberry fruits are relatively small (about ¼ inch, 0.5 cm in diameter). Depending on the cultivar, expect to pick from the middle to late summer in New England but much earlier elsewhere.

Rabbiteye blueberry

The rabbiteye blueberry (*Vaccinium virgatum*; zones 6 to 9) is a larger, more heat-tolerant species that exhibits broader soil adaptation than highbush blueberries. Native to the U.S. Southeast, it and its selections are well adapted to southern climes; plants are relatively susceptible to cold injury, too tender to survive in colder climates. Compared to a highbush blueberry, most people find the fruit a bit smaller in size and the flavor a touch sweeter, though the skin can be tougher. In the wild, this species makes an enormous bush, often reaching 20 feet (6 m) in height; available cultivars are more compact. The name reportedly comes from the observation that the berries are as pink as a white rabbit's eye—before ripening, of course. Note: for pollination of rabbiteye blueberries, you must plant two different cultivars.

Half-high blueberry

The half-high blueberry (zones 3 to 7) is the result of a cross between northern highbush blueberry (*Vaccinium corymbosum*) and lowbush blueberry (*V. angustifolium*). Developed in Minnesota for production in very cold regions, these plants are more than hardy: most of their fruiting area is below the snowline, which protects them from even the most extreme cold temperatures. Half-high blueberries are low-growing bushes, generally between 1 and 4 feet (0.3 and 1.2 m) tall. This makes them an attractive choice as a landscape plant, not to mention a good option for container planting.

Yield is not quite as bountiful as that of the northern highbush cultivars, but the half-highs are a wonderful alternative in harsh climes. The "wild" flavor and berry quality of these hybrids can be quite good. Ripening occurs in mid to late summer. All have vivid foliage color in the fall.

CHOOSING THE RIGHT CULTIVAR

It is important to pick a type of blueberry that performs well not just in your hardiness zone but in your region. For best fruit production, you'll want to put in at least two different blueberry cultivars for cross-pollination purposes. You can even select several cultivars, choosing so that your garden provides an ongoing harvest from midsummer through fall. But if need be or when your space is limited, don't worry—you can still get a significant crop with only one cultivar

'Bluecrop'

(unless your choice is a rabbiteye, in which case you must have a second cultivar for pollination).

No matter how big or small your blueberry ambitions are, research your choice. Seek a cultivar or cultivars known to perform well in your area. Talk to neighbors who grow berries. Contact your local Cooperative Extension personnel for their opinion and recommendations. Ask any local farmers who raise blueberries what they suggest. But remember that as a home gardener, you are free to focus on taste rather than yield, fruit size, or other characteristics. Go for a cultivar that is reputed to have better-than-average flavor; 'Jersey', 'Legacy', and 'Spartan', for instance, are hard to beat for rich, aromatic blueberry flavor. Keep in mind, too, that all blueberries taste better if they are left on the bush until fully ripe (for more details, see "Harvesting and After-care," later in this chapter).

Some of the tastiest cultivars may have limiting characteristics to contend with, unfortunately. Some have lower fruit yield, or a less favorable growth habit (more spreading, or even drooping). A bit of good news is that blueberry breeders are increasingly sensitive to the call for substantial, sweet taste. Many are working on improving flavor, not only by using the best selections of the northern highbush blueberry but also by incorporating other species that are inherently more flavorful. Thus, newer introductions are always worth considering—keep an eye out for them, or track them down at specialty fruit nurseries.

Use the recommendations in the cultivar lists as guidelines only: as always, your particular growing region or microclimates in your own yard may allow you to explore beyond those listed.

Northern highbush blueberries

'Aurora' **NE NW** Very late. Berries are large, light blue, flattened, and firm. Very good, sweet flavor. People tend to pick 'Aurora' too early; flavor is poor if the fruits are not left to hang until fully ripe. Bush is vigorous and productive but squatter than most northern highbush plants. Prune to encourage upright growth in your plants while they're young.

'Bluecrop' **NE MW NW SW** Midseason. Bush is vigorous and upright. Fruit is medium-sized, firm, and has good flavor. Shows consistently high production and good cold hardiness. Season tends to be prolonged. Berries appear to be ripe (completely blue)

'Bluegold'

'Bluejay'

'Duke'

well before full sweetness is achieved, so wait until the full blue color is present. Taste a few to be sure. Foliage turns bright red in the fall.

'Bluegold' NE MW NW Mid to late season. Abundant crops of medium-sized berries with excellent flavor and firmness. A compact, roundish, low-growing plant with many branches; tops out at about 4 feet (1.2 m) high. Yellow to red-purple fall color.

'Bluejay' MW NW Early to midseason. Bush is vigorous, upright, and open. Long-stemmed berries hang in loose clusters, remaining on the bush without loss of quality until most are ripe. Fruit is medium-sized, firm, and light blue. Wood and buds are resistant to low winter temperatures, but flowers are less resistant to frost than those of 'Bluecrop'. Production is sometimes erratic. Fall leaf color is orange and yellow.

'Blueray' NE MW Early to midseason. Plant is very vigorous. Fruit is borne in small, tight clusters that can cause berries to drop, especially in hot weather. Berries are medium-sized, soft, and dark blue with good flavor. Consistently productive, but may overproduce if not pruned properly. Upright-spreading habit. Very hardy. Fall foliage is bright red to bright yellow.

'Bluetta' MW Very early. Forms a short, compact, low-spreading bush of medium vigor. Fruit is small, soft, and blue-black with fair flavor. Berries can hang on for a long period. Not a heavy yielder; consistency of production may be a problem. Winters well, and does not break dormancy too early. The main reason to grow it is its earliness.

'Chandler' NE MW NW Mid to late season. Especially big berries with robust flavor—in fact, it's the largest-fruited blueberry available! Ripens over a long period, up to six weeks—a real plus. Slightly spreading growth habit; fall foliage is spectacular shades of orange to wine-red.

'Coville' SE MW Late. Very vigorous, moderately spreading bush with open fruit clusters. Berry is large, medium blue, highly aromatic, and tart. Moderate yields; fruit-set problems can limit productivity. Narrow soil adaptation.

'Darrow' NE MW Late. Large, fair to good quality, somewhat tart, slightly flattened, juicy berries in abundance. Plant habit is upright. Fall leaf color is orange and red.

'Earliblue'

'Elliott'

'Jersey'

'Draper' NE MW NW SW Early to midseason. The standard in this season. Sweet, firm fruit with good flavor. Blooms late, which protects flowers from late spring frosts, but ripens early. Compact plants never get that large but are still very productive. Fall foliage is orange to yellow.

'Duke' NE SE MW NW SW Very early. Blooms late, avoiding late frosts. A vigorous, upright bush that bears medium-sized, firm, light blue fruit. Fruit flavor is appealingly mild, with a nice sweet pop. Plant has numerous canes that are stocky and moderately branched. Buds and wood tolerate fluctuating winter temperatures well. Harvest can be completed in two or three pickings. Does not like "wet feet."

'Earliblue' RM Very early. Forms a very vigorous, upright-spreading bush. Fruit is large, soft, and light blue with fair flavor. Fruit does not drop easily when ripe. Not a heavy yielder.

'Elliott' NE MW Very late. Bush is vigorous and upright. Productive, hardy, and disease-resistant. Berry is medium-sized and light blue in color, with firm flesh and only fair flavor; can be tart. Berry may be fully blue when not fully ripe. Interplanting with another late-blooming cultivar provides cross-pollination and improves size and flavor. Red to orange fall foliage.

'Hardyblue' NW Midseason. Produces lots of dark blue, soft, medium-sized, aromatic, sweet berries. Adapted to many soils. Plant is upright; fall color is bright red.

'Jersey' NE MW RM NW Late. Vigorous, tall (to 8 feet, 2.5 m), erect bush with open fruit clusters. Medium-sized, moderately firm fruit with good color and good flavor, considered by some to be the sweetest of all cultivars. May have fruit-set problems; can set small fruit without pollination. Orange fall foliage.

'Legacy' MW NW SW Midseason. Vigorous, upright plant with somewhat willowy canes. Very productive, with large, firm, blue fruit with outstanding flavor. Widely adapted, except for areas with very cold winters.

'Liberty' NE MW NW SW Midseason. Bush is 7 to 8 feet (2 to 2.5 m) tall, vigorous, and productive. Large crops of firm, light-colored, juicy berries; they tend to be soft in hot weather. Fall color is orange to red.

'Patriot'   'Rubel'   'Spartan'

'Patriot' NE MW RM Early. Plant is upright and compact; good for a small garden or even a large container. Fruit is medium in size, soft, and tart. Developed in Maine, it has excellent cold hardiness, but early bloom is susceptible to frost damage. Fall foliage is fiery shades of red, orange, and yellow.

'Rubel' MW NW Mid to late season. Bounty of small, firm fruit; said to have the highest antioxidant level of any blueberry! Bush is erect, 4 to 6 feet (1.2 to 1.8 m) high, and very productive. Fall color is bright red.

'Spartan' NE MW NW SW Early. Plants are vigorous, upright, and open; berries are large, fairly firm, light blue, and highly flavored. Fussier than most about growing conditions—performs poorly on soils that don't drain well or have a high pH. Blooms late, which helps prevent frost injury. Autumn leaf color is orange and yellow.

Southern highbush blueberries

'Emerald' SE Early to midseason. Reliable and productive. Plant is 5 to 6 feet (1.5 to 1.8 m) tall, with a handsome, rounded, spreading growth habit. Fruit is quite large, with mild, sweet flavor.

'Jewel' SE SW Early to midseason. Especially popular in California thanks to its adaptability and tolerance of heat. Big crops of very large, tangy, juicy fruit. For best pollination, plant with a midseason cultivar.

'Jubilee' SE MW Midseason. An upright plant, to about 6 feet (1.8 m), with yellow to wine-red fall foliage. Berries are abundant, medium-sized, and sweet. Tolerates summer heat, heavier soil, and sudden winter cold better than most.

'Misty' SE MW Early. A good-looking landscape plant, 4 to 6 feet (1.2 to 1.8 m) high, with a somewhat spreading habit, blue-green foliage in spring and summer, burgundy in fall. Fruit is medium to large, spicy-sweet, light blue. Particularly heat-tolerant.

'O'Neal' SE Very early. Exceptionally delicious large berries, very juicy and sweet, medium blue color. Vigorous plants are 4 to 6 feet (1.2 to 1.8 m), upright, spreading; fall color is bright orange to wine-red.

'Sharpblue' SE Early. Abundant fruit is medium to large in size, dark blue, with good flavor. Plant habit is semi-upright. Best in mild winters where frosts are rare.

'Star' MW Early. Good yields on vigorous bushes. Fruit is large, firm, and sweet.

'Powderblue'

'Sunshine Blue' SE NW SW Mid to late season. A compact, semi-dwarf plant, generally no more than 3 feet (1 m) tall—so, well suited to patio and deck containers. Tolerates higher-pH soils better than many of its kin and has very low chill requirements. Berries are medium-sized and sweet.

Lowbush blueberries

'Burgundy' NE MW Midseason. Hails from Maine, so very cold-hardy. Low-growing enough to be used as a groundcover—habit is wider than tall. A plant known for its distinctive foliage, which shifts over the seasons from bronze to gray-green to gorgeous, deep burgundy in fall. Produces small, tasty, light blue berries.

Rabbiteye blueberries

'Bluebelle' SE Early to midseason. Large, dark blue, tasty berries over a long period. Plant habit is upright.

'Climax' SE SW Early. Most berries ripen in a short period of time; they are small to medium, firm, with good flavor. Plants are productive and have an open, upright habit and good fall color. Widely planted; recommended for California's Central Coast.

'Ochlockonee' NW SW Very late. Medium to large, bright blue berries of very good quality, as they lack the thick skin and grit cells of most rabbiteyes. Large, vigorous plants. Standard in the West as a pollinizer for 'Powderblue'.

'Pink Lemonade' NW SW Midseason. The top-selling rabbiteye, thanks to its unique, bright pink fruit. Medium-sized, sweet fruit. The upright plant is attractive and produces a moderate crop.

'Powderblue' NW SW Very late. Rabbiteye standard in the West. Medium to large, bright blue berries that lack the thick skin and grit cells of most rabbiteyes. Large, vigorous plants.

'Premier' SE Early to midseason. Ripens with or ahead of 'Climax'. Medium to large berries have pleasing flavor and color. Plants are vigorous and productive, with an upright growth habit.

'Tifblue' SE Mid to late season. Large, firm, light blue berries grow on a vigorous, upright, productive bush; nice fall color. More cold-hardy than most rabbiteyes.

'Northland'

'Vernon' SE NW SW Early. Flowers late, after 'Climax'. Large, firm berries can hang ripe on the plant for several days. Bred in Georgia; blueberry enthusiasts in mild-climate areas of California take note.

Half-high blueberries

'Chippewa' MW NW Midseason. A compact, upright bush with bright red fall color. Berries are largest in this category, sky-blue in color, and sweet-flavored. Very cold-hardy.

'Northblue' NE MW RM NW Early to midseason. Short, upright cultivar with moderate yields. Fruit is dark blue, firm, and juicy, with good tart flavor. Leaves are particularly ornamental in the fall, turning a lovely dark burgundy-red. Especially cold-tolerant.

'Northcountry' MW RM NW Midseason. Medium-sized fruit is sweet and mild and seems to be closest to what people think of when they think of wild flavor. Bush reaches only about 3 feet (1 m) in height.

'Northland' NE MW RM Early. Very productive with medium-sized fruit. Fruit can be soft. Canes are flexible and can be weighed down by snow. Generates a large number of canes.

'Northsky' NE MW NW Midseason. Bush is less than 3 feet (1 m) in height and has dense branching. Fruit is light blue; great for fresh eating, also stores well. Has lovely dark red foliage in the fall.

'Perpetua' NW First double-cropping blueberry: plants flower and ripen fruit in June and then flower in July for an August-to-frost crop. Small-fruited, like a lowbush type. Plant is compact with lustrous dark green foliage that contrasts very nicely with its white flowers. A beautiful ornamental that will produce some pancake berries for you and fruit for the birds into the fall.

'Polaris' NE MW RM NW Early. A good choice for colder areas where early ripening is desired. Fruit is medium-sized, delicate, and very sweet. Plant is compact yet upright, attaining no more than 4 feet (1.2 m) in height; fall color is bright red.

'Top Hat' NE MW Midseason. A compact, dense plant that produces abundant white flowers and small, light blue berries. Grows only 12 to 24 inches (30 to 60 cm) high and wide, with curving branches. An excellent choice for a border planting, container culture, or even a bonsai project.

SITING AND PLANTING

Happy, productive blueberry bushes need to have their basic needs met. Devote an appropriate area to a row, or try a grouping. Invest in good plants, get them off to a good start, and the payoff will be good and plenty! Blueberries grow best in an open, sunny area, in ground that is moist, porous, and—especially—acidic. It's best to pick out a site ahead of time and get it ready. You'll want to eliminate any noxious weeds and add organic matter. Depending on where you garden, you may also need to lower the soil pH—that is, make it more acidic.

Light and soil requirements

Full sun is best for blueberries, for the health and growth of the plants as well as to inspire plentiful fruit. That means six to eight hours of unobstructed light per day during the summer months—more is even better. That said, blueberry bushes will still manage and produce in some shade, but growth will be lankier and yields will be lower.

The primary limitation of blueberries in the landscape is their requirement for acidic soils. You really want to give them a spot with a pH between 4.5 and 5.5. Higher than that, and they will struggle: a high pH makes certain important nutrients, most notably iron, unavailable. For an accurate reading, invest in a soil test. If it turns out that your soil's pH level is not low enough, you can nudge it with amendments—the lab will send you appropriate recommendations about what (and how much of it) to add.

Organic gardeners like sulfur. Here's an idea of how much of it you may need to add (in pounds per 100 square feet, 30 m_2) to three different soil types (sand, loam, and clay) to reach a desired pH of 4.5:

Present pH	Sand	Loam	Clay
6.0	1.2	3.5	3.7
6.5	1.5	4.6	4.8
7.0	1.9	5.8	6.0
7.5	2.3	6.9	7.1

Note that sulfur is slow-reacting in soil, although the more finely ground it is, the more quickly it will act. Add it the summer or fall before you install your blueberry bushes; work on a windless day, so it doesn't drift away. And be careful: more than the recommended amount is not better and, indeed, can cause more harm than good.

You should also dig in plentiful organic matter, a worthy idea for any garden crop. The higher the organic content, the more acidic the soil can be without suffering nutrient deficiencies. Good, rich compost is ideal. Bear in mind that blueberry plants have relatively shallow root systems, so there is no need to dig deeply. You should be safe

Once you have your young blueberry bushes in the ground, give them a good soaking to get them off to a good start.

preparing ground to a depth of 1 foot (30 cm). Well-drained soil is best.

Buying plants

Get healthy two-year-old blueberry plants from a reputable nursery; they are usually offered in polybags or potted. Such small potted blueberry plants are often more pricey than bare-root plants, but they work best. Younger plants, such as year-old rooted cuttings, grow more slowly and will take much longer to reach fruiting size; plants that are more than three years old are more expensive and, honestly, not worth the extra cost.

Planting day

In cold climates, blueberries should be planted in early spring in soil that was prepared the previous season. Fall planting is even better in climates where winter frost-heaving is not a problem, as the plants have the chance to get a good root system established while above-ground parts of the plant are dormant. Either way, work on an overcast or not extremely hot day to minimize stress for your young plants.

When planting two-year-old potted plants, dig planting holes that are about two times the diameter of the root ball, and place the plants slightly deeper than they were growing in the nursery. Create a basin around the base of each one, so that when you water, it sinks into the root area rather than running off. There's no need to do any cutting back of the topgrowth, since the root system is only minimally disturbed. However, if a plant is potbound, tease apart and break up the roots with your hands and spread them outward as you maneuver them into place in the hole. Water well afterward.

When planting two-year-old bare-root plants, remove any flowers and 50 to 60 percent of the wood immediately after planting. This helps them become established.

Don't crowd your blueberry bushes. They need room to reach their mature size, plus you want to have easy, comfortable access for pruning—and picking!

Planting plans

If you are putting in a row of blueberries, space young plants 3 to 6 feet (1 to 1.8 m) apart. If you are planting more than one row, allow as much room as you need between rows, typically 8 to 10 feet (2.5 to 3 m).

If you are adding a few plants to a shrub border or mixed garden bed, just give each one several feet of elbow room on all sides (the expected mature size of the plant should be on the tag, or the nursery where you got it can tell you). It's never a good idea to crowd the plants.

Blueberries in containers

Want only a plant or two? Have a sunny patio or deck? Have totally unsuitable soil—it's alkaline, and everyone tells you you'll never grow blueberries? Good news: growing blueberries in a container is easy and satisfying. Their naturally shallow root systems, easy-going nature, and potential longevity make it work. Here are some tips for success.

Pick a cultivar that is naturally small or dwarf in size. Lowbush and half-high blueberries are perfect. Lowbush blueberries are so compact they could even work as a tabletop centerpiece, like edible bonsai almost, while half-high types ought to go in a bigger container (such as a 10-gallon pot).

Like blueberries grown in the ground, container-grown plants need a pH around 4.5. So fill a big pot with an acidic soilless growing medium, such as a combination of 80 percent fir bark, 10 percent peat moss, and 10 percent perlite. Or use mostly sphagnum peat moss (dampen it first). Add some sand, which adds weight to the pot and facilitates drainage.

Be diligent about water. Plants in containers dry out, especially if exposed to drying winds or long hours of hot sunshine. The root zone needs to stay moist!

Finally, protect your potted blueberry plant from winter cold. The roots of blueberries grown in the ground are somewhat

You can raise blueberries even if your space is limited. Just provide them with ample containers and situate them in a sunny spot. Depending on your local bird population, you may still have to put netting over them when the fruit is ripening.

protected by the layer of earth and possibly snow above them. In containers, however, the shallow roots are touching the edges of the pot on all sides, and cold temperatures are directly transferred to them. You could choose a cultivar rated perhaps one zone colder. Alternatively, when freezing weather looms, wrap your dormant plant up, pot and all, in burlap, old sheets, blankets, or even bubble wrap. Or sink pot and all into the ground out in your yard somewhere, then mulch well. Plants in containers on the West Coast will overwinter just fine outdoors.

CARING FOR YOUR PLANTS

Mulching

In most areas, it is very beneficial to mulch your blueberry plants. Mulch is key to achieving a healthy planting and good, consistent yields, as it helps the soil retain water and minimizes fluctuations in soil moisture. A protective covering of mulch also thwarts sprouting weeds, which means it will save you time weeding, down the line.

After planting, apply a 4-inch (10-cm) layer of mulch around the base of the plants. Hardwood bark mulch (such as that used for landscaping), rotted sawdust, and even

Use soaker hoses to save yourself time and effort in supplying your blueberry bushes with the consistent water they need.

chopped corncobs are all fine; don't use leaf mulch, as it can mat down and prevent water from getting to the roots. Replenish mulch when it breaks down over time, or rain washes some of it away.

Watering

Water your blueberry plants thoroughly immediately after planting. Blueberries require at least an inch (2.5 cm) of water per week during the growing season and even more, up to 4 inches (10 cm) per week, during fruit ripening. Blueberries growing in sandy soils will require more water than those growing in soils with a higher water-holding capacity.

Hand watering with a hose will get the job done; however, soaker hoses and drip or trickle irrigation systems will supply the plant with more uniform watering while simultaneously conserving water. The drip line can be placed on the soil or under mulch so that it is out of the way and, in some cases, semi-permanent. Soaker hoses are ideal: not only do they target the moisture to the plant, but they guarantee water deliveries are regular and consistent.

Fertilizing

Contrary to what you might think, or what you might do for other garden plants, you should *not* fertilize new blueberry plants after planting. The young roots are just getting their feet under them and are vulnerable to burning from fertilizers. Every spring going forward, though, it's a good idea to give your blueberry plants a dose of sulfur, to keep the soil in the 4.5 to 5.0 pH range. Sulfur is a safe, natural fertilizer that acts slowly when applied properly and watered in well; find it as elemental sulfur, sulfur powder, iron sulfate, or ammonium sulfate (go easy with this last: it is prone to dropping the pH too low too fast).

Farmers who raise blueberries commercially add a little more sulfur each year, starting with 4 ounces (115 grams) per plant in year two and working up to 8 ounces (225 grams) per plant by year six and beyond—you can emulate this regimen if you wish. Alternatively, you can use a commercial fertilizer specifically labeled for acid-loving plants (blueberries, heaths and heathers, azaleas and other rhododendrons).

Never use a fertilizer that includes potassium chloride, which adversely affects blueberries. And never fertilize your blueberries late in the growing season or in the fall. This inspires fresh, succulent growth that risks being damaged by the coming colder weather.

In any event, keep an eye on your blueberry plants as the years go by. Nutrient deficiencies show up as poor growth, light green or red leaves in the summer, and, of course, poor yield. If any of these symptoms appear, your best bet is to re-do the soil test, then follow the recommendations.

PRUNING

Left to their own devices, blueberry plants become overgrown and less productive. You should intervene and keep them well pruned. Pruning is best accomplished toward the end of the dormant season, in late winter or early spring. Do not prune in the fall months, however, as this can compel a plant to produce new shoots that risk being killed by winter cold. You should remove any dead or damaged canes as soon as you notice them.

The philosophy behind pruning blueberries is to constantly renew the plants by cutting out the older, less productive canes, thus forcing new ones to develop from the base of the plant. Your pruning not only controls crop load and thus increases fruit quality, it also invigorates the plant as a whole.

Let the first two years be spent establishing the plant's frame and root system. In year one, remove all flower buds in order to force vegetative growth. These are easily recognizable during late dormancy, as they are found on the tips of the canes and are

If you let your blueberry bushes grow with abandon, they get too dense, and berry production drops significantly.

The best time to prune a blueberry plant is before it leafs out in early spring. At this time, it will recover more quickly from the cuts and soon surge into a new season of growth.

plumper than the vegetative buds. In year two, remove *some* of flower buds, again to encourage sound establishment. Sacrificing this small amount of fruit is well worth the dividend of establishing a planting that will fruit for 50 years or more if well maintained.

Blueberry branches are most productive when they are between two and four years old, offering a balance of abundant fruit and good fruit size. As branches age, you will notice that berry size tends to dwindle, and some cultivars get so tall or highly branched that they are difficult to manage. If a plant is properly pruned, it will replace old canes with new, and a majority of its branches will be in a productive intermediate stage.

Once a blueberry plant is mature (six to eight years old), it should produce at least three to five new shoots per year. By pruning out the weakest and most congested of these new canes, you will be left with two or three each of new, one-, two-, three-, and four-year old canes, or 10 to 15 total. Take out criss-crossing twigs while you're at it. After, the center of the plant will be more open. Please note that the production of new shoots is cultivar-dependent; some do not respond as well to pruning as others. Here are some recommendations for specific blueberry pruning situations:

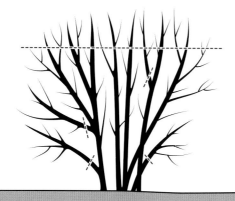

An unpruned blueberry bush, with dashed lines indicating where to make major cuts.

A properly pruned blueberry bush.

- Plants with an open or spreading growth habit ('Chandler', 'Coville'). Try to keep these plants growing more erectly than is their tendency. Concentrate pruning on the outer edge of the bush, pruning any drooping lateral branch back to the main stem.
- Plants with an erect or upright habit ('Bluecrop', 'Elliott', 'Jersey'). These plants tend to become very dense in the center, and the resulting shade reduces shoot formation and flower bud initiation. Keep their centers from becoming too dense: remove the older central canes, and prune excessive inward-pointing laterals back to the main canes of the plant.
- Plants that are very vigorous ('Blueray', 'Earliblue'). While removing some canes is needed on all cultivars, do so more forcefully with these selections. Focus on removing whole canes at the base of your plants, rather than detail pruning.

- Plants that are weak or slow-growing ('Bluetta'). Treat weak-growing cultivars the opposite of how you do the vigorous ones: focus on detail pruning, rather than removing whole canes at the base. Where many laterals ("twiggy" growth) have formed, remove half of them at pruning. Systematically remove the weaker laterals (those less than ⅛ inch, 0.25 cm in diameter); this will improve berry quality.

Revitalizing old blueberry bushes

Perhaps you find ancient blueberry plants on a property you have just purchased, or you have not been able to keep up with pruning, and your plants have become overgrown and wild-looking. If they are more than 6 feet (1.8 m) tall, have a lot of gray or dead wood in the center, have a lot of branching of the canes, or have no new growth coming up from the base, chances are they need some rejuvenating. This work is best done at the end of the dormant season, as winter is ending but before spring brings fresh new growth.

Begin by cutting back about half of the canes at the base. Then prune the remaining canes to a height of no more than 6 feet (1.8 m). If the remaining canes have a lot of fine, twiggy, highly branched wood, selectively prune out the smallest shoots (always cutting them back to the larger shoot to which they are attached), thus allowing the remaining shoots greater access to water, nutrients, and light.

After all that chopping, a "snack" is a good idea. Give each plant about 8 ounces (225 grams) of ammonium sulfate. Then cover the root area with 2 to 3 inches (5 to 8 cm) of mulch (such as rotted sawdust), keep them watered, and you're off and running. You should see considerable new shoot production that same year. After that, remove about 20 percent of the old canes per year and perhaps some of the more straggly new canes until you have established the desired plant form.

HARVESTING AND AFTERCARE

Depending on where you garden and which blueberries you have chosen, the harvest begins strong and very early with cultivars such as 'Duke' and 'Earliblue' and has the potential to continue all the way through mid-autumn with 'Elliott' and the rabbiteyes (in the South). A mature blueberry plant—again, depending on conditions and cultivar—can easily produce 7 to 30 pounds (3 to 14 kg) of fruit per year. There are, however, some tricks of the trade.

Picking

Berries turn blue three to four days *before* they attain maximum sweetness and flavor, so let them hang. In fact, commercial growers often wait until a few berries fall to the ground before they begin to harvest. It's not easy to resist the temptation to pick such luscious-looking fruit, but remember that the great thing about growing fruit in your backyard is that you *can* wait for the best moment.

Look closely. When the fruit is ripe for picking, it will be blue all the way around. Don't forget to check the back of the fruit before you roll it off the plant. The area around the stem (pedicel) that connects to the fruit will be the last to ripen; if the berry is not quite ready, this area will still be green or reddish, and you might have to come back in a few days to try again. One great thing about blueberries, as compared to other berries, is that you don't have to rush to harvest. The ripe berries can remain on the plants for several days, or longer, without spoiling.

Fresh-picked blueberries, if placed in the refrigerator immediately upon harvest, will

Harvesting blueberries on a warm summer day is one of life's great delights. Just be careful to pick only ones that are fully blue.

store well for seven to 10 days. Alternatively, you can put them directly into the freezer (Ziploc bags or other plastic containers work perfectly) and make them into jams or pies at some later, colder, more convenient date.

Overwintering

Like any garden shrub, blueberry bushes have hardiness ratings that you should heed. If you selected a cultivar that is borderline hardy where you live, take steps to help it through a cold winter with minimal damage.

Don't prune until late winter—that only inspires fresh growth that can be harmed by freezing temperatures. But tidy up around the plants, removing plant debris and obviously dead stems. Then lay down 2 to 3 inches (5 to 8 cm) of mulch over the root zone to moderate soil temperatures and prevent frost-heaving.

Frosts in late winter and early spring can rob you of your homegrown berries and damage your plants (browned leaves, mainly). You can take action to prevent

THE BLUE BLOOM

As blueberries begin to turn blue, they develop a glaucous coating (you may have observed something similar on plums and some apples). What is it? It is *not* the residue of a spray product, chemical or otherwise, nor is it an indication that your berries have some sort of plant disease. This thin waxy coating is completely natural: it keeps the berries waterproof and helps to retain their internal moisture longer. So don't try to wash this bloom, as it is known, off. Certainly don't try to remove it before freezing your harvest, or the berries will turn into hard little pellets.

Blueberry fruits, as they begin to color up on the road to ripening, develop a protective waxy coating, or bloom.

harm, such as spreading sheets or frost blankets over your plants. Though frost usually is toughest on opened flowers, in the case of blueberry, it can also cause injury to the small green fruits. All this is a good argument for choosing at the outset a cultivar or cultivars suitable for your climate zone.

TROUBLESHOOTING

When blueberries are grown in a sunny site with soil that pleases them, they have relatively few insect and disease pests. An exception is if you happen to be located near a large population of blueberries in commercial production. The large monocultures are too attractive for the pests to ignore, and if your planting is within an easy jaunt, either by wind or wings, the pests will come. Weeds are likely to be a problem one way or the other, but you can easily escape the disease and insect assault if you are gardening in an isolated area.

New and healthy plantings have the best success rate when it comes to avoiding pests. Weakened plants are much more likely to succumb to cane diseases and are also more likely targets for mites and aphids.

Sometimes damage to your plants—browned leaves, dying-back twigs, damaged blossoms or developing fruit—is not the fault of a disease or insect pest, but rather due to frost damage. In order to avoid a mis-diagnosis and possible panic, check your local weather reports and protect vulnerable bushes as described in the previous section.

Fungal diseases

Canker diseases (notable pathogens: *Fusicoccum*, *Phomopsis*, and *Botryosphaeria* spp.) can all damage blueberries. They most often affect plants that are already weak from other stresses, but these fungal cankers can also harm healthy plants. Remove canes that show symptoms at pruning, or as they appear. Get the prunings out of the area and burn them.

Fusicoccum canker manifests itself as small red spots that may enlarge into bull's-eye-like marks on the canes. Look for the signs when you are dormant pruning, and remove affected canes. In phomopsis and botryosphaeria cankers, shoots wilt as new growth emerges in the spring, and then dry up and often curl. Prune and destroy any canes that show these symptoms, being sure to cut the canes down to where the pith is no longer brown.

Mummy berry (pathogen: *Monilinia vaccinii-corymbosi*) is a fungal disease that afflicts new shoots, flowers, and fruit. Shoots and leaves will turn brown and wilt as they emerge, and flowers may also appear to be brown and water-soaked. Infected flowers that are left to fruit will form berries that are tan in color. These will shrivel, turn reddish buff to gray, become hard, and are completely inedible.

If you see any mummy berry in your planting, take action! The fungus overwinters on the ground, so clean up around your plants at the end of the season and/or rake in early spring. Remove and dispose of ruined berries and other debris to break the cycle. Then prune and weed around your planting to improve air flow.

Common pests and other problems

Many insects that attack a wide range of plants also attack blueberries. Japanese beetles are much more fond of roses and raspberries, but given the chance, they may zero in on your blueberries. Gypsy moths, in years when they are abundant, can be problematic. Low numbers of these insects will not cause much difficulty, but if numbers become very high, you could use insecticides such as Bt (*Bacillus thuringiensis*), a naturally occurring bacterium (sold under several names, including Dipel); follow label instructions regarding amount and timing to the letter. Here are a few other pests and problems more specific to blueberries.

Blueberry maggot (*Rhagoletis mendax*) is very common in the northeastern and north central United States. These small larvae are white maggots. Only one larva will attack each fruit, but unfortunately the infected fruit stays on the plant and you may have the extreme displeasure of biting into it. Keeping plants cleared of overripe fruit will help avoid this problem.

In the unlikely event that you end up with a heavy infestation of these guys, you can try placing yellow sticky traps (baited with ammonium acetate or ammonium carbonate) around the perimeter of the planting. Living with the constant anxiety of "does this berry have a maggot in it?" is just not an option!

Cranberry fruitworm and **cherry fruitworm** render blueberries useless in the eastern United States. Cranberry fruitworm (*Acrobasis vaccinii*) damage is characterized by fruits that are webbed together, and the presence of the worm's frass (excrement) in the webbing. The cherry fruitworm (*Grapholita packardi*) is a little more insidious. This worm enters the fruit and systematically consumes all the contents inside the skin, leaving only its frass in exchange. Your blueberries will turn blue prematurely, and may also have some webbing. If you press open such a fruit with your fingers (please don't bite into it), you will find only dry frass.

If either of these insects becomes a serious problem, they can be controlled with Bt at petal fall and again ten days later. For specifics, contact your local Cooperative Extension Service office.

Spotted wing drosophila (*Drosophila suzukii*), a problem with other berries, appears to be a problem for blueberries, too, in some places. If you garden in a climate that is on the damp side, your plants may be vulnerable (drier areas and areas with warmer temperatures are less susceptible to this pest). These are small vinegar flies, like fruit flies in size—adults are about $1/16$ inch long. The wings of the males have a black spot toward the tip. Females lack this spot but have a prominent, saw-edged ovipositor for getting their eggs into your fruit. Spotted wing drosophila (SWD) attacks healthy, ripening fruit, as well as already split or damaged berries, and you may not notice the damage until you begin to pick. Telltale signs include soft berries with brown spots; these can then exude juice. Diagnosis might be complicated if other insects or bacterial infection move in on the heels of SWD damage. The fruit cannot be eaten—it contains eggs and/or maggots.

For home gardeners, the key is early detection. First, set out traps (a yogurt cup baited with apple cider vinegar and a drop or two of liquid soap to break the surface tension, so the flies can drown) near your bushes to confirm that these pests are present. Monitor your plants carefully and pick berries as soon as they ripen. Check over the harvest carefully and dispose of damaged blueberries (in your trash; composting will

Get out, get out! If birds have access to your blueberry bushes, they'll strip the plants of all those delicious berries. Don't let this happen—cover the plants with netting before the berries start to ripen.

not kill these). If this pest becomes a serious concern for you, seek out exclusion nets meant for keeping it out; such nets will also keep birds at bay.

Birds. There is a pest that makes any blueberry grower shudder. Whether one or many, they can completely consume a crop before it is ripe, or even more dishearteningly, the crop can be devoured a few days or minutes before harvest. The heinous criminal? *Birds*. Birds simply adore blueberries and will consume them with greedy delight. The suspect species vary by location, but the most common culprits are starlings, robins, and cedar waxwings.

Netting is the one and only way to control bird damage. Nothing else—bird alarm devices, suspended owls, inflatable snakes—works well enough to be considered a solution. So, bite the bullet and buy some netting.

Put it on—gently, as blueberry branches

Do not allow weeds in your blueberry patch. Aside from the obvious reason that these unwelcome plants are competing with your berry bushes for the same resources, some weeds, notably dandelions, may harbor viruses that can be transmitted to your plants by nematodes in the soil.

can be brittle—before the fruit starts to ripen. Make sure that the netting is tied securely around the base of the canes to exclude rodents as well as the birds. Your best bet, honestly, might be to erect a frame around and over the bushes, draping the netting thoroughly over that. Make it out of wood or PVC pipes. Don't forget to anchor or seal all the edges; you'll be amazed not only by how hard some birds will try to get in anyway, but by how much havoc even one or two birds can wreak if they succeed.

Weeds. Weeds can be a problem in blueberry plantings, particularly if they are not dealt with regularly. The blueberry has an advantage over the lowly strawberry here by virtue of its height; it takes a tall weed to compete with a highbush blueberry plant for sun. On the other hand, blueberries are not especially adept at taking up water, particularly when the soil is cold, and weeds can easily rob them of the continuous supply of water upon which they thrive.

Many gardeners think that mulching will protect their blueberry plants from any weed problems, but it's important to remember that not all mulches are created equal. Hay, for example, often contains weed seeds. Instead, suppress weeds by mulching with hardwood bark, rotted sawdust, or chopped corncobs.

FOR THOSE WHO long equally for garden-fresh fruit and a fairly easy time of attaining it, blueberries are a great choice. No bending, no elaborate pruning or training, no thorns to contend with—you can look forward to naturally tidy, moderately sized bushes laden with delicious berries. The single biggest issue is providing the plants the acidic soil they relish—that, and outcompeting birds for the harvest.

Blueberries have the added advantages of being fairly tough, trouble-free plants for edible landscapes in most areas, handsome even when they are not heavy with fruit. Glossy green leaves are spangled with little white flowers in spring and, come fall, cooler weather turns the foliage vivid shades of red. These are reasons enough to convince someone with not much spare garden space to try a plant or two. But the big draw remains the splendid, healthy fruit. Picked at its peak, warmed by the sun and bursting with succulent sweetness, a blueberry really is the essence of summer.

specialty berries

SPECIALTY BERRIES—GOOSEBERRIES,

currants, elderberries, and other so-called minor berries—are grown commercially only on a limited scale. And while it should be remembered that most "major" horticultural crops were once minor (the now-familiar highbush blueberry was something of a novelty as recently as 1950), most of these specialty berries haven't hit the big time due to specific limitations such as excessive thorniness (many gooseberries) or flavor that must be processed to be appreciated (black currants and elderberries). Often they are merely misunderstood or under-appreciated because of our collective inexperience with them.

Generations of gardeners have prized elderberries for their easy growth and beneficial berries, and cultivars selected for improved fruiting and ornamental traits are now available.

And even though breeders have increasingly taken an interest in them, the general public still doesn't know much about them. Growing these berries is an opportunity for you to explore new territory, so to speak. It's also fun to cultivate something that may simply be unavailable at your grocery store or even favorite farmers' market.

GOOSEBERRIES AND CURRANTS

Gooseberries and currants have long enjoyed great popularity in Europe. In the 1800s, more than 700 gooseberry cultivars were available on the continent, and gooseberry clubs were established by enthusiasts. Most cultivars of the European *Ribes uva-crispa* bore large and sweet fruit as a result of centuries of selection and breeding, whereas American gooseberries derived from *R. hirtellum* had less desirable (sour) flavor but more resistance to disease. The gooseberries grown nowadays (northern Europe is the main region of production) are primarily hybrids of these American and European types, offering good flavor and varying degrees of disease resistance. Even fruit wimps eat these little morsels fresh, and gooseberries are often cooked into jams,

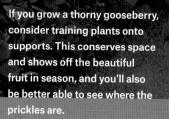

If you grow a thorny gooseberry, consider training plants onto supports. This conserves space and shows off the beautiful fruit in season, and you'll also be better able to see where the prickles are.

Currant bushes are not that bulky, comparatively speaking. You can fit them into smaller spaces and look forward to a satisfying harvest.

pies, and other desserts. They have been enthusiastically touted on *The Fabulous Beekman Boys*, a popular Cooking Channel reality show featuring Josh Kilmer-Purcell and Brent Ridge (who describe a gooseberry's taste as "tart green apple crossed with a plum"). If you run an Internet search, you'll find their recipes and many others, including some revivals of long-ago favorites like gooseberry fool (a sweet-tart pudding) and gooseberry pie. Tempting!

Currants too make delicious jams, jellies, syrups, chutneys, sorbets, and even wines and liqueurs, on their own or combined with other fruits or spices. Black currants (*Ribes nigrum*)—a novelty at best in the United States—are commonplace in Canada and other countries, valued for their high vitamin C content, especially in places where citrus is not grown. Black currant juice fills the niche in the United Kingdom, Poland, and New Zealand that orange juice or Concord grape juice fills in the United States. Red currants (*R. rubrum*, *R. sativum*, *R. petraeum*) and white currants (a type of red currant) are also available. Last but not least is a North American native, the clove currant (*R. aureum* var. *villosum*); this one is spangled with spicily scented yellow flowers in spring.

Some people say that if you let currants hang on the bush long enough (or if you

Where space is limited, currant plants may be fan-trained to a wall.

have a taste for the tart and tangy), they are just fine for fresh eating. Definitely not for everyone, but feel free to give it a try and acquire the taste! As to dried currants, it is very difficult to find ones that are really currants: most commercially available dried "currants" are in fact tiny raisins made from dried 'Zante'/'Black Corinth' grapes. True dried currants are smaller and seedier, and have a very different flavor. Classic scone recipes call for these (though raisins are usually substituted), and currants may also be used in everything from stuffed grape leaves to pork dishes. The best way to dry them yourself is to use a dehydrator.

Gooseberry and currant shrubs are 3 to 6 feet (1 to 1.8 m) tall at maturity. Gooseberry plants tend to be thorny and usually have a more spreading habit, while currant bushes are always thornless and have a more upright profile. And surely no fruit is more beautiful than red currants. They truly look like little dangling jewels; their visual appeal alone is reason enough to grow them.

ABOUT THE PLANT

Gooseberries and currants are often spoken of together because they are in the same genus. Traditionally, they have been considered members of the saxifrage family; more recently, their entire genus *Ribes* has

Alternatively, you can line up some perky currant bushes along a fence.

Many gooseberries are greenish; some are more yellow, and others are closer to red. Flavor, not surprisingly, varies according to cultivar, so try a few before making your selection.

been moved by botanists into its very own family, Grossulariaceae. Family ties aside, a few noteworthy differences distinguish them from each other.

Gooseberry fruits are larger, ranging from a pea to a large grape in size. They are borne singly or in small groups along the stems of the plant. Individual berries can be slightly fuzzy and/or have crisp skin, but the flesh inside is juicy. When ripe, gooseberries come off the plant easily. Color varies from greenish yellow to pink or red.

Currant fruits, on the other hand, are smaller, usually pea-sized or less, have a more melting texture, and may need a taste test to determine ripeness. Currant flowers,

and thus the subsequent fruits, are carried in long, often heavy, drooping clusters, or strigs. Ripe currant fruit color varies depending on the cultivar.

Gooseberry plants can be wickedly spiny, though this characteristic varies by cultivar (less threatening ones are available), whereas currants are always spineless. They also differ in leaf shape: gooseberries have fairly small, slightly frilly leaves; currant leaves are much larger, with three distinct lobes and coarse serrations. Currants also have aromatic (not to say pungent) foliage, which you will notice most when pruning or picking.

Unlike other fruiting plants, gooseberries

Currants carry their fruits in great long clusters, or strigs. You can simply clip the entire strig at harvest and strip off individual berries later indoors.

Some currants are bright red, some are inky blue or black, some are pink or white. Flavor ranges from sharply tart to grape-sweet, so do some homework before deciding which one you'd like to have.

and currants tolerate and even produce fruit in partial shade. Generally speaking, both gooseberries and currants perform optimally in areas with cooler summers and colder winters, where their buds can obtain necessary chilling while dormant. They don't perform well in the South or Southwest. These hardy plants do best in zones (3)4 to 7.

Finally, most plants in the genus *Ribes* are self-fertile, meaning that planting additional plants or different cultivars to boost fruit production is unnecessary. If a cultivar is not self-fertile, however, the nursery will alert you and recommend that you buy the additional plants needed for adequate pollination; black currants, for example, produce better when you grow two or more different varieties.

CHOOSING THE RIGHT CULTIVAR

The gooseberry cultivars listed here tend to weather powdery mildew and leaf spot diseases better than others. Those with a mostly North American background have more natural resistance but, unfortunately, also less interesting fruit flavors. The

ILLEGAL PLANTS? THE "CURRENT" SITUATION

Confusion as to the legality of growing gooseberries and currants has reigned since a federal ban prohibited their production in the United States. The ban was established because *Ribes* plants can serve as alternate hosts to *Cronartium ribicola*, the fungus which causes white pine blister rust, a very serious and debilitating tree disease. Along with the ban, from 1944 to 1966, a program to wipe out native *Ribes* species was also in effect.

Cronartium ribicola needs both a five-needled pine such as eastern white pine (*Pinus strobus*) and a *Ribes* plant to complete its life cycle. It harms the berry shrubs (premature defoliation, usually) but doesn't tend to kill them; however, it can prove fatal to the pines, particularly young trees or ones under stress. Implicated in particular are cultivars of the black currant, *Ribes nigrum*, a European species (the fungus was in fact introduced to North America via imported European pine trees); less of a threat are the clove currant (*R. aureum* var. *villosum*), red currants, and gooseberries. Lawmakers in some states recognize this, and allow cultivation of gooseberries and red currants but not black currants; laws of other states, where five-needled pines are economically important, prohibit all *Ribes* plants.

The federal legislation was rescinded in 1966, not because the disease was conquered but because eradicating an entire genus proved difficult and ultimately did not appear to be a lasting control. Transporting infected pines has been an issue that has nothing to do with gooseberries and currants, for instance. Since 1966, it has been up to the states to decide whether to "allow" these potential Typhoid Marys; a handful of states maintain their bans, for example, North Carolina and Maine. So, if you wish to grow currants or gooseberries, find out what your state and local ordinances are. If they do not prohibit growing *Ribes*, go ahead. If you have white or other five-needled pines nearby, however, please seek out and plant only resistant species or cultivars. Research is ongoing (there are now, for example, resistant black currants); ask your nursery for an update.

European types usually have larger and better-flavored fruit than American cultivars, but they tend not to be as resistant to mildew. Green-fruited ones are said to be the sweetest, reds are more tart, and pink gooseberries are somewhere in between—though, of course, your crops and taste may vary.

Currant cultivars are available in three colors: red (to pink), black, or white. For most folks, currants are not for fresh eating but for eye-candy as they develop and for processing, when ripe, into wonderful juices or jellies.

Prospective *Ribes* growers should consult with other gardeners in their area and/or contact their nearest Cooperative Extension Service office for the most up-to-date information on cultivars for their location.

Gooseberries

'Amish Red' NE MW NW Midseason. Medium-sized red fruit. A very productive, large plant of American origin. Wonderful resistance to mildew.

'Black Velvet' NE MW NW Midseason. Dark red fruit; excellent sweet flavor. A vigorous grower with less-daunting single thorns. Good resistance to mildew and other diseases.

'Hinnonmaki Red'

'Invicta'

KEY TO REGIONS

NE = Northeast, including southern Quebec and southern Ontario
SE = Southeast, including Gulf Coast
MW = Midwest and Great Plains, including adjacent Canadian provinces
RM = Rocky Mountain/Mountain West
NW = Pacific Northwest, including Northern California and British Columbia
SW = Southwest and Southern California

'Captivator' NE MW NW Mid to late season. Pink to red fruit is teardrop-shaped and sweet. The plant, a cross of American and European cultivars, is mildew-resistant and has a blessedly low thorn count.

'Careless' NE NW Midseason. Abundant crops of relatively large, yellow to pale green, somewhat elongated, firm fruits. The flavor has been described as "delicious and refreshing!" Plant habit is spreading, tending to few branches. Mercifully few thorns. Susceptible to mildew. A cultivar of British origins.

'Downing' NE RM NW Midseason. Hardy and prolific, it produces tough-skinned pale green fruit that is, frankly, quite tart and most often used for processing. Makes a beautiful chartreuse-colored jam. An older cultivar, of North American background.

'Early Sulphur' (**'Yellow Rough'**) NW Midseason. A strong, erect bush with few bristles. Slow-growing and slow to come into bearing, but the deep yellow, hairy, pear-shaped fruits are delicious. Another British cultivar; does get mildew.

'Glenndale' MW RM NW Midseason. An old and vigorous cultivar with serious spines but good disease resistance. The fruit is dark red to purple and has good flavor. Best for processing rather than out-of-hand eating. Mixed background (*Ribes missouriense* × *R. uva-crispa*).

'Hinnonmaki Red' NE MW NW Midseason. One of the best-flavored (tart skin, sweet flesh) and highest-yielding gooseberries. True to its name, the ripe fruit is a deep ruby-red. Thorny, upright plant. Some mildew resistance.

'Hinnonmaki Yellow' NE MW NW Midseason. The yellow-green fruit is somewhat variable in shape and has especially sweet flavor relative to other gooseberries. The bush is substantial and, yes, quite thorny.

'Invicta' RM NW Early to midseason. Bears generous amounts of fairly large, green, tart gooseberries. They are difficult to pick, however, because it is a super-thorny bush—bring gloves. A mildew-resistant cultivar of British origin; moderately resistant to white pine blister rust.

'Langley Gage' NW Midseason. Large white berry, described in one catalog as "too delicious for words." Bush is dense and of medium size. From Britain.

'Oregon Champion' RM NW Midseason. Forms a tall bush with a weeping habit; very spiny. Berries are small and pale, turning greenish yellow on maturity. An heirloom American cultivar (thought to be a cross between 'Crown Bob' and 'Houghton').

'Poorman' NE MW RM NW Early to midseason. Sweet, flavorful, aromatic red fruit is medium-sized; texture is on the softer side. Considered the best cultivar for American gardens. It forms a sturdy, vigorous bush and is highly productive. Not as spiny as some. North American background.

'Red Jacket' RM NW Late. Medium to large green berry with a red blush and decent flavor. A very strong, upright plant with some mildew resistance. The spines are less obtrusive than some. Fruit is easy to harvest because it hangs well below the branches. Of American origin.

'Tixia' ('Rafzicta') NE MW NW Midseason. Large, bright red, elongated, rather smooth fruit. A strong grower with few thorns; these are mercifully very soft on the tips. Developed in Switzerland.

'Welcome' NE MW RM NW Early to midseason. Pink to red, medium-sized, flavorful fruit. Canes are initially weak and spreading but become more vigorous and erect as the plant matures. Nearly thornless. Bred in Minnesota.

'Whinham's Industry' NW Midseason. Tasty red berries are large and thick-skinned. Upright growth habit; tolerates shade well but can get mildewy. An old British favorite.

Currants

'Ben Lomond' (black) MW RM NW Midseason. A black currant with excellent fruit quality. Forms a robust yet compact plant with good yields of relatively large fruit. It is susceptible to mildew as well as white pine blister rust, though, so cannot be grown/is prohibited in some areas. Very popular in its homeland, Scotland.

'Ben Sarek' (black) NE MW RM Early to midseason. This one produces abundant crops of large, easy-to-pick black currants (pick promptly, however, as hang time is less than most). Plant habit is compact, between 3 and 4 feet (1 and 1.2 m) tall. Good resistance to white pine blister rust and mildew, as well as frosts. Another Scottish cultivar.

'Blanka' (white) NE MW NW Midseason. A so-called white currant (fruit is actually

'Ben Sarek'

'Pink Champagne'

'Red Lake'

light yellow); begins tart but becomes mildly sweet. Large, heavy clusters—one of the most prolific, most reliable producers among currants. Growth habit is vigorous, loose, and spreading. Mildew-resistant.

'Crandall' (red) NE MW NW SW Late. A selection of the clove currant, *Ribes aureum* var. *villosum*. It ripens later in summer and is productive, with tasty, glossy black fruit (alas, not as high in anthocyanins as its European cousins). Disease-resistant plants, 4 to 6 feet (1.2 to 1.8 m) high and wide.

'Jonkheer van Tets' (red) NE MW RM NW Early. A good red currant from Holland. May need frost-protection or a warmer microclimate in your yard. Produces a bounty of medium-sized fruit with excellent flavor. Plant habit is upright. Mildew-resistant but very susceptible to cane blight.

'Pink Champagne' (pink) NE MW NW Midseason. Aptly named! Medium-sized fruit is light pink and delicious; yields are not large, but for some, it's still very much worth growing. Plant is vigorous and upright in habit. Resistant to leaf diseases, including mildew.

'Red Lake' (red) NE MW RM NW Midseason. A vigorous, hardy, and productive red currant. The good-quality, juicy fruit is large and bright red. The long clusters are easy to pick. Vulnerable to mildew, however.

'Rovada' (red) NE MW NW Late. A good choice for areas where frosts linger, therefore. Red berries are large and abundant and carried in especially long clusters; flavor is outstanding. Plant habit is upright, to 5 feet (1.5 m) tall. Resistant to mildew and other leaf diseases, but susceptible to cane blight. Hails from the Netherlands.

'Titania' (black) NE MW RM NW Midseason. A large black currant with immunity to white pine blister rust (however, double-check with your nursery and/or local Cooperative Extension Service agent). It has good mildew resistance as well. Plants are large and vigorous, and the fruit is best suited to juice.

'Wilder' (red) NE MW RM NW Early to midseason. A bright red currant very much like 'Red Lake'—high yielding, with good-quality berries—but fruit is slightly smaller and ripens earlier, and the plant is mildew-resistant and has greater resistance to leaf spot.

Even a single gooseberry plant is worth growing, if you can find a good, sunny spot for it in your garden. They never get big and rangy, they don't sucker, they respond very well to basic care, they're good-looking, and—let's not forget—they reward you with tasty berries.

SITING AND PLANTING

Gooseberries and currants do not require a lot of space in your yard. Sure, you can site them along a property line or make a low to medium hedge with them, if you wish. But one or several plants clustered in an appropriate spot can do just fine, growing and producing with basic care. And either one of these woody shrubs would work well clustered irregularly around foundations or in the center of a larger island planting.

The right spot

Because gooseberries and currants prosper in a spot with good drainage, some gardeners have found that planting them on a slight slope is perfect—assuming it's convenient for you.

Remember also that gooseberries are spiky and thorny, so you'll probably want to put them where only you (not other, non-gardening family members, visitors, or pets) have to worry about that. Currants can be grown where you might place any other average-size shrub. Bear in mind, however, that neither type of plant is especially attractive in flower or foliage (generally, not even fall color is very dramatic). You are growing these for their fruit. Thus, many gardeners place them out near other fruit plants or adjacent to the vegetable or kitchen garden.

These and all plants in the genus *Ribes* are best not planted anywhere near five-needled pines (see the sidebar on page 164 for the "current" situation) because they serve as an alternate host for white pine blister rust. Scientists have determined that 1,000 to 3,000 feet (300 to 915 m) is a safe distance, but don't chance it. Grow resistant cultivars, if any at all, if five-needled pines are in your own yard or adjoining properties.

Diseases that afflict gooseberries and currants are generally fungal and appear as damage to the leaves, so the chosen site should have good air circulation.

Light and soil requirements

Like all fruit plants, gooseberries and currants thrive in ample sun. Unlike some of the other fruits, though, they can tolerate partial shade and still produce well. If your summers are hot, these plants are best sited in filtered shade, or a spot where they get morning shade. Don't forget to mulch to keep the roots cooler. Temperatures in the high 80s cause them to falter and drop

leaves, and/or the fruit can sunburn.

As for soil, you ought to get it tested and amended a year prior to planting. These plants like rich, well-drained ground with a pH of between 6 and 7.5 (about 6.5 is ideal). If your soil is too acidic, they won't be able to take up the nutrients they need to thrive. Add powdered garden lime or dolomitic limestone, sold at garden centers and home-improvement outlets. Alternatively, bonemeal might do the trick. How much should you dig in? That depends on how many plants you are getting ready for and the results of your soil test.

In general, it is a good practice to amend the soil at the planting site with compost (decomposed manure is perfect, cow or chicken) prior to planting and via side-dressing every spring. Your gooseberry and currant bushes will appreciate it. This habit improves soil texture and fertility over time and should also boost the harvest.

Buying plants

Get strong, well-rooted one- or two-year-old dormant gooseberry or currant plants from a reliable nursery; they are usually offered in polybags or potted. When you go shopping, check to make sure the young plants you are considering are showing no signs of stress, disease, or insect pests.

Nurseries that sell *Ribes* plants keep up with current regulations relative to white pine blister rust—or should—so be sure to identify where you live and garden when inquiring or ordering. These currants await their fate and your careful inspection and approval.

Although currants are not as bulky or tall as some other berry plants, they still appreciate their own patch of garden space. Clear out weeds and don't place them too close to neighboring plants.

Planting day

Currants and gooseberries initiate growth very early in the spring, so you should plant them in the fall or early spring. Before planting, remove any damaged roots. Also, trim back the top portions of each plant to 6 to 10 inches (15 to 25 cm), leaving three to six well-spaced branches. Plant them as deep as they were growing at the nursery, and water in well.

Planting plans

If you're putting in only a single plant, give it elbowroom of at least 3 to 4 feet (1 to 1.2 m) in all directions. Such a siting allows beneficial air flow and room for future growth. In the case of the thorny gooseberries, you'll also be glad to give them a buffer zone as a warning or reminder to yourself and others to be careful in their vicinity. Alternatively, they can be espaliered or raised in containers, or some dense and thorny gooseberries, such as 'Glenndale' or 'Poorman', could be used to form a thick hedge that does not spread via root suckering.

If you'd like to install a grouping or row of gooseberries or currants, space plants 3 to 4 feet (1 to 1.2 m) apart; currants can be placed a little more closely, while gooseberries may want a little more space. Rows should be a good 6 to 8 feet (1.8 to 2.5 m) apart.

If space is limited, you could site a few cultivars against a wall or fence, raising your plants as cordons. This involves a little extra pruning and training. Basically, each early spring you identify and shorten one upright stem, back to about 6 inches (15 cm) of new growth, and shorten any laterals.

CARING FOR YOUR PLANTS

Mulching

After planting, and going forward, it's a good idea to mulch around the base of your plants to help conserve soil moisture and keep weeds at bay. Lay down 2 to 3 inches (5 to 8 cm) of straw, decomposed sawdust, dried grass clippings, or wood chips.

Once your gooseberry or currant plant is in the ground, lay down a good organic mulch.

Watering

Ribes plants are not especially greedy for water, but neither are they drought-tolerant. What they need is consistent moisture in well-drained ground—ideally 1 to 2 inches (2.5 to 5 cm) of water per week, from rainfall or, if necessary, from you. During very hot spells at the height of summer, don't wait for them to show distress before irrigating. Give them deep soakings from a trickling hose. Be forewarned that ripening gooseberries can sunburn if their soil dries out.

Fertilizing

There is no need to feed your plants their first year, assuming you've prepared the soil properly. But even when a site's soil is organically rich, and even when you side-dress with more compost each spring, your gooseberries or currants may still be "hungry." Give them whatever plant food you would give any woody plant or fruit tree. At a minimum, fertilize annually early each spring, just as growth is starting. Apply your favorite organic plant food or between 5 and

At a minimum, it's a good idea to give your gooseberry or currant bushes a nice side-dressing of compost once a year, in early spring after growth is underway.

Although it sounds counterintuitive, it's recommended that you remove flower buds or flowers in your plants' first season in your garden. This frees up the plants to devote their energy to establishing strong root systems. The payoff harvest will come in their second season.

8 ounces (140 and 225 grams) of a balanced 10-10-10 fertilizer in an 18-inch (45-cm) ring around each plant.

PRUNING

Although you may be eager for a specialty harvest, it's a good idea to hold off for a year and let your new gooseberry or currant plants become established first. Therefore, when they bloom that first spring, come by with the clippers and remove all the flowers, or at least the majority. The plants will then invest important effort in root development and growth that you'll be glad for in the second year and beyond.

The basic aim of pruning gooseberries and currants is to develop and then maintain an open, vase-shaped profile that allows you access for picking but leaves some branching to prevent the potential for sunburn. The branches should be fairly evenly spaced and not cross or rub against one another—in other words, don't let a bush become twiggy and congested.

The best time to prune these is while they are still dormant, in late winter or early spring. Clip out canes that are trailing or have dropped on the soil. Also remove those that shade out the center of the plant. Aim to take out all but six or, at most, eight of the most vigorous shoots to become the upcoming season's bearing canes. Maintain this in subsequent years, always taking out older canes (which have dark brown bark) and letting new ones replace them.

Gooseberries, and currants, are best pruned when not actively growing, in late winter or early spring. In this way, you can clearly see—and contend with—the canes, and the plants will recover and begin growing as the days get longer and the air and soil warm up.

Wear heavy protective gloves when pruning prickly, thorny gooseberries.

HARVESTING AND AFTERCARE

With a good site and good care, well-established *Ribes* plants of all kinds can fruit for 10 to 15 years or more. Here's how to get the most out of your plants.

Picking

Gooseberries and currants ripen their fruit, generally speaking, over a two- to three-week period in spring to midsummer. Unlike some fruits, these won't go bad if left on the plant for a while, but on the other hand, don't wait too long or the fruit will rot and fall to the ground, which would be a shame.

Well-colored fruits should be harvested as they appear. Gooseberries will come off easily when ready. But don't forget to bring sturdy gloves. Even cultivars that are touted as having smaller, fewer, or softer thorns can still be tricky to work around.

Determining when to pick your currants is not always as simple. Depending on the cultivar(s) you are growing, color will vary. For these, taste! It's easiest to take off entire clusters of currants when you feel they are ripe. You can cook the entire strig if you're making jam, jelly, juice, and similar items, straining out or extracting the stem afterward. Do remove any leaves beforehand, though.

Expect each mature, healthy plant to produce 5 to 7 pounds (2 to 3 kg) of fruit, usually by the third or fourth year.

Currants are ready to pick when they color up, but you might want to taste a few first to make sure. The longer they remain on the plant, the sweeter they get.

The best way to pick ripe gooseberries is with some protection for your hands. Mimic this gardener's clever method: grasp the prickly plant with a gloved hand, and remove the small berries with your free hand.

Overwintering

Both gooseberries and currants are fairly winter-tough plants, surviving winters into zone 4 and sometimes even zone 3, depending on the cultivar.

TROUBLESHOOTING

While generally pretty easy-going, gooseberries and currants can have a few issues, depending on growing conditions. You can head off problems by investing in good, healthy plants and working to keep them that way. If certain plant diseases are a problem in your area, seek out resistant varieties. Also and as always, make it a practice to be a tidy gardener. Clean up around the base of your plants every fall, so diseases and other pests can't lodge or overwinter in fallen leaves and other plant debris. Take out damaged and dead growth whenever you see it, and cart it away.

Fungal diseases

Powdery mildew, leaf spot, and anthracnose (pathogens: *Podosphaera mors-uvae*, *Mycosphaerella ribis*, and *Drepanopeziza ribis*, respectively) are common fungal diseases found on currants and gooseberries, and as mentioned, all susceptible *Ribes* can fall prey to white pine blister rust. In general, powdery mildew is less of a problem on currants compared to gooseberries, but currants are more susceptible to white pine blister rust.

Preventing these problems is not difficult. Start out by selecting resistant cultivars. Choose a site with good air flow and keep the bushes properly pruned, again, to encourage good air circulation.

Liquid lime sulfur—available at garden centers and farm supply stores—can be used for controlling mildew. It is relatively low in toxicity though admittedly smelly. It should be applied when plants are at the green-tip stage of bud development (this is just what it sounds like: when the leaf tips are just showing green) and again two to three weeks later, after bloom. Horticultural oil may also do the trick; consult your local Cooperative Extension Service office for complete recommendations if you decide to go this route.

Common pests and other problems

Currants and gooseberries are vulnerable to various pests; here are a few. If you still have trouble identifying and coping with something attacking your plants, please get in touch with your local Cooperative Extension Service office for help.

Currant borer and **gooseberry sawfly** are two common pests. The currant borer (*Synanthedon tipuliformis*) tunnels through the pith of the cane, causing the leaves on afflicted canes to turn yellow. The small, spotted, caterpillar-like larva of the gooseberry sawfly (*Nematus ribesii*) can strip young leaves down to nothing but midrib and vein; the entire bush becomes alarmingly defoliated. Prevent the pests from getting to plants in the first place by covering the bushes with well-secured floating row covers. If you miss that opportunity and detect a small infestation, hand-picking and destroying the tiny worms offers some measure of control, or you can try spraying with soapy water, insecticidal soap, or Bt. But if there are many, act decisively. Remove and destroy any infected canes. For those gardeners willing to go beyond low-impact, organic control measures such as these, there are foliar insecticides; again, seek the advice of your local Cooperative Extension Service agent before proceeding.

Currant stem girdlers (*Janus integer*) have paid a visit if you see new shoots drooping and wilting in the spring. You will likely find evidence of small larvae in the cane below the flagging shoot. The best control is simply to remove and destroy all infested shoots.

If raiding birds turn out to be a problem, cover your *Ribes* bushes with netting while the berries are ripening.

If the leaves of your *Ribes* plants start to look blistered, suspect aphids. Luckily, these are easy to combat in the home garden if you notice them early.

Currant fruit fly (*Euphranta canadensis*)—also called the gooseberry maggot—can be a problem. The first part of its life cycle occurs in the soil; adults emerge in spring and lay eggs on forming fruit; these later hatch as maggots, which feed on the berries from within. If you correctly identify this culprit in your garden, you can block a key stage in its life cycle. Lay old towels or tarps on the ground around your plants in spring to prevent the flies from entering the soil to pupate in the first place. Alternatively, cover the bushes in spring with floating row covers so the flies can't get to them.

Aphids sometimes invade. Telltale damage is crinkled, blistered leaves. Look closely—they congregate on the underside of leaves.

Dislodge them with a stiff spray from the water hose.

Birds. Yes, birds like gooseberries and currants; they have none of the human hesitation about the tartness of fresh berries. In particular, robins adore pink gooseberries and black currants. Netting is the best protection; drape or support the protective covering so that there is some space between the netting and the plant, so the cleverest marauders can't just reach right through. Bird alarms, including noisemakers, might also help keep these pests away.

Weeds. As is the case with so many other prized garden plants, weeds can sneak in on the wind or even in a nursery pot, and soon compete for the same resources of soil

Elderberry fruits are richly colored and laden with healthful benefits. Note the attractive contrast between the dark berries and the red stems on which they are carried.

nutrients, light, and water. Don't let this happen to your gooseberries and currants. Maintain a good mulch around their bases, and yank out or use a sharp hoe on invading weeds.

ELDERBERRIES

Elderberries (*Sambucus* spp.) are shrubs in the honeysuckle family (Adoxaceae) with myriad uses. Their stems—hollow tubes from which the pith is easily removed— have served as pipes (to tap sugar maples,

among other uses), straws, and flutes; in fact, the genus name derives from *sambuca*, a kind of flute so ancient it is said to have been favored by Pan. The flowers ("elder-blow") have been used medicinally, steeped as tea, to soothe fevers and alleviate allergies. Both the flowers and fruit are used to make dyes, and the bark and roots are rich in tannin, which was once used to tan leather. The native American elderberry, *Sambucus nigra* subsp. *canadensis*, is often seen growing wild, to 10 to 12 feet (3 to 4 m) high and wide—an impressive plant with bountiful,

'BLACK BEAUTY' AND BEYOND

Fashions come and go in the landscaping world; recently, there's been skyrocketing interest in elderberries as ornamentals. Horticulturists have capitalized on the plants' natural variability, and you can now find a variety of forms valued solely for their attractive leaves and flowers.

Thinner- and cut-leaved cultivars have been likened to Japanese maples, with the advantages of being faster-growing and more cold-hardy. Examples include 'Dart's Greenlace' and 'Laciniata'.

Light green to chartreuse-leaved cultivars have novel appeal. Examples include 'Aurea' and 'Sutherland Gold' (whose berries are toxic: it is a selection of *Sambucus racemosa*, a nonedible species).

Dark-leaved cultivars are gorgeous, especially when paired to dramatic effect with light-colored flowers and foliage in mixed borders and perennial beds. 'Black Beauty' has rich purple leaves and pink flowers; 'Black Lace' is similar, but its foliage is even more deeply dissected. Both are derived from the European *Sambucus nigra*.

Variegated cultivars always add interest. *Sambucus nigra* 'Marginata' has white variegation; 'Madonna' has yellow variegation. These are not as vigorous as their plain-green-leaved counterparts, but they are still sturdy plants.

Sterile-flowered cultivars have larger, more showy blooms (but alas, no berry harvest). 'Plena' offers an abundance of fully double white flowers; 'Rosea Plena' is the pink version. 'Maxima', a European cultivar, carries its huge white flowers on purple pedicels.

umbrella-like white flowerheads. It also suckers readily, which can be a bonus or a hassle, depending on where you have placed it. It is hardy in zones 3 to 7(8). The typical European species, *S. nigra*, can get even bigger and more tree-like, to 20 feet (6 m) high and wide; North American gardeners have found it to be hardy in zones 4 to 7(8). It blooms earlier and has pink flowers. Both produce shiny dark purple fruits.

The berries are not often eaten fresh because of their uniquely tart flavor and relative seediness; they are usually made into pies and jellies. Some folks prefer to remove most or all of the seeds, a task easily accomplished by straining the cooked fruit through several layers of cheesecloth. Elderberries also make a great, healthful juice and an interesting wine. The flowers too can be soaked with citrus juice, tartaric acid, and sugar to extract the aromatics and make a wonderful non-alcoholic summertime beverage. But please note: the leaves, bark, stems, and roots of all elderberries should not be ingested; they contain toxic cyanogenic glycosides.

Elderberries are also appreciated as garden ornamentals, either as tall upright shrubs that grow in suckering clumps of individual canes (if it is the North American subspecies) or as a specimen with a single trunk (usually so, if the European species). Install several side by side as a hedge, or scatter them as a background or foundation planting behind shorter plants. In the fall, the leaves of some turn an attractive red.

Bountiful elderberries are preceded by large white flowerheads that can cover the plant in early summer.

ABOUT THE PLANT

Elderberry leaves are pinnately compound, with five to 11 leaflets averaging 5 inches (13 cm) in length with finely serrate margins. The root system is fibrous and shallow, so cultivation should be shallow. Clusters of pleasantly scented flowers are 3 to 10 inches (7.5 to 25 cm) across.

Individual fruits are quite small, but they are borne on large, umbrella-like inflorescences. The berries are not only tasty but beneficial: their ascorbic acid (vitamin C) content is the highest of any garden fruit except for black currants. They also have significant amounts of vitamins A and B, as well as compounds thought to improve heart

Unlike most other small fruits, elderberries are borne on the current season's growth, on the terminus of new shoots. Therefore, winter injury to the flower buds is not a concern.

health and boost the immune system. People prone to urinary tract infections sometimes prefer elderberry juice to cranberry juice; its most common use, however, is to prevent or treat the common cold.

Elderberries are considered partially self-fruitful, but production goes way up with cross-pollination. In the wild, this occurs naturally. In a garden setting, simply plant more than one cultivar.

CHOOSING THE RIGHT CULTIVAR

The cultivars listed here are all derived from the American elderberry. All are only partially self-fertile, so, again, it is beneficial to plant two or more different ones together for better yield.

'Adams' NE SE MW RM NW Late. The oldest cultivar. Vigorous and productive, with large fruit clusters and berries held aloft on strong branches. Ripens in early September. Gets about 10 feet (3 m) high and wide.

'Johns'

KEY TO REGIONS

NE = Northeast, including southern Quebec and southern Ontario
SE = Southeast, including Gulf Coast
MW = Midwest and Great Plains, including adjacent Canadian provinces
RM = Rocky Mountain/Mountain West
NW = Pacific Northwest, including Northern California and British Columbia
SW = Southwest and Southern California

'Bob Gordon' MW Mid to late season. Large berries, large yields. When it begins to mature, the head inverts, thus reducing bird damage. Originally collected in the wild in Missouri.

'Johns' NE SE MW RM NW Mid to late season. A vigorous plant that produces 10- to 12-foot (3- to 4-m) canes in fertile soils. It ripens about 10 days earlier than 'Adams' and is a favorite for making jelly.

'Nova' NE SE MW RM Midseason. Berries are larger and sweeter than those of 'Adams'. It lacks the astringency of some varieties. Relatively compact, only about 6 feet (1.8 m) high and wide.

'Samdal' NE SE MW RM Midseason. A vigorous newer cultivar, hailing from Denmark. Its large fruit clusters are valued for jellies, pies, and wine-making. (Sister cultivar 'Samyl' is recommended for cross-pollination.)

'Scotia' NE SE MW RM NW Midseason. Berries have a higher sugar content than other cultivars, and the bushes are somewhat smaller.

'Wyldewood' MW Midseason. A well-tested cultivar from the University of Missouri. A vigorous producer, the first elderberry to reach budbreak in spring and the latest to ripen. Up to three fruit clusters per stem.

'York' NE SE MW RM NW Late. The largest berries of any cultivar, borne on a compact bush, about 6 feet (1.8 m) tall.

SITING AND PLANTING

And another great thing about elderberries? They are particularly easy to grow. Given a sunny site and decent soil, they have few pest problems, are vigorous, and give freely of their many riches. But it's not true that elderberries will tolerate lousy soil, or prefer soggy ground. For good-looking, productive plants, you want to site them in well-drained soil that is organically rich.

The right spot

If the spot you have in mind is presently overgrown with weeds, it is particularly important to prepare it ahead of time—at least one season, if not one full year, before planting. Otherwise, the weeds can really cause problems for your new plants, stealing away water and nutrients from their shallow young root systems and making it difficult for them to become established. Plant a cover crop, or till and solarize the area beforehand.

An open area is really ideal, not just for sunshine but because good air circulation makes for healthier growth. Nearby woods or weeds can also increase the chances of problems from insects, diseases, and birds.

Last but not least, pick a spot that is not too close to smaller plants or garden treasures, because happy elderberry plants sucker and spread, forming colonies over time. While you can—and should—do some maintenance pruning (more on that ahead), you don't want to sign up for a constant battle over garden real estate. Give these plants room to grow.

Light and soil requirements

Full sun (six to eight hours daily) is best for growing elderberries, although they will tolerate some shade. As for soil, they are not fussy and can grow in anything from sandy ground to clay loam. However, slightly acidic soil (pH between 5.5 and 6.5) is best.

Buying plants

Although elderberry plants are propagated easily by stem cuttings (hardwood or softwood), viruses are sometimes a problem in the wild, so it is best to purchase plants from a reputable nursery. They are generally available as rooted cuttings. Pick out at least two different cultivars; cross-pollination improves productivity.

Planting day

Plant in early spring, after all danger of frost is past and the soil is workable (not mucky). Create a basin around the base of each baby plant, then water them in well their first day, and beyond if rainfall is sparse.

Planting plans

Set young plants 5 to 7 feet (1.5 to 2 m) apart in a row, with a minimum of 10 feet (3 m) between rows. If you are after a bountiful crop of elderberries, you've already acquired more than one; for successful cross-pollination, plant your two cultivars no more than 60 feet (18 m) apart.

CARING FOR YOUR PLANTS

Mulching

You'll want to protect those shallow roots from drying out and keep competing weeds at bay, so be sure to mulch. Two to 3 inches (5 to 8 cm) of straw or bark chips should be sufficient.

Watering

Elderberries have a shallow root system, so be sure to keep them well watered during the first season. Consistent moisture is important!

Fertilizing

There is no need to fertilize the first season. A hearty side-dressing of compost, delivered early every spring afterward, is beneficial. If you prefer commercial fertilizer, apply a mere 2 ounces (55 grams) of ammonium nitrate per year of the plant's age (up to no more than 1 pound, 0.5 kg per plant) in a ring around the base, again, in early spring. It's never a good idea to overfeed these plants, or you'll get lush vegetative growth at the expense of flowers and, consequently, berries.

PRUNING

Each year, healthy elderberry plants usually produce several new canes, which attain their full height during that first year. The two-year-old canes with several lateral branches are most fruitful, so you want to be sure to retain plenty of these. Overall, just keep after the older, less productive, and diseased or damaged canes, if any, taking them out every year in late winter or early spring at ground level. If you don't keep up with maintenance pruning, your planting can become an overgrown, unproductive thicket.

HARVESTING AND AFTERCARE

Picking

Fruit is ripe when dark purple, usually in mid-August to mid-September, depending on the cultivar and where you garden. Elderberry plants produce a small crop in the first year after planting. They should reach full production in three to five years, offering 12 to 15 pounds (5 to 7 kg) of fruit per plant per year. Fresh berries are very tart; processed ones have a sweet, earthy flavor.

Harvest by cutting the clusters and gently stripping the fragile berries from the stems. An even easier method is to freeze entire clusters in plastic bags overnight, then drop the bag on the floor the next day; all the berries will break off of the clusters cleanly. Then simply pour the berries off and discard the (toxic, remember) cluster stalks. Fresh elderberries don't keep well at room temperature, so refrigerate immediately. Freeze or process shortly thereafter.

Overwintering

In colder areas, a late-autumn application of mulch is a good idea, to moderate soil-temperature fluctuations and to prevent frost-heaving of the shallow root systems. European elderberry and the cultivars derived from it are less hardy and sometimes die back to the ground in colder areas. No

Black chokeberry

Black chokeberry

worries—they should resprout from the roots the following spring.

TROUBLESHOOTING

Fungal diseases such as stem and twig cankers (notable pathogens: *Cytospora*, *Nectria*, and *Sphaeropsis* spp.) can infect elderberries, but these can be effectively controlled by removing and burning afflicted wood. Other common pests and problems follow.

Elder shoot borer (*Desmocerus palliatus*) may cause dieback and cane loss, but infested canes can be simply removed and burned. These pests tend to target older canes, which you should be taking out regularly anyway.

Birds. Many songbirds adore elderberries, from finches and jays to sparrows and cedar waxwings. Pigeons, grouse, and pheasant will also eat the berries. In fact, birdwatchers sometimes plant elderberries in order to attract certain species to their yards. The plants are prolific enough that you can afford to share some of the bounty.

Weeds. Weeds are a threat to young elderberry bushes because they compete for the same resources; it is important therefore to clear the area prior to planting and to keep a good mulch in place going forward, to keep weeds from returning. Because tomato ringspot virus can be a problem on elderberries, it is especially important to control weeds around the root zone; this virus naturally resides in such common weeds as the dandelion and is transmitted by soil nematodes, so removing the weeds removes a primary source of infection.

MORE SPECIALTY BERRIES

Black chokeberry (*Aronia melanocarpa*, *Photinia melanocarpa*; zones 3 to 8). This medium-sized, suckering shrub reaches about 6 feet (1.8 m) at maturity. In spring, it is covered with white flowers; by fall, these

Cranberry

Cranberry

become blueberry-sized, deep purple berries, which look great against the often fiery red foliage. It prospers in colder climates and adapts to most soils. Best of all, plants are care-free: diseases and other pests do not trouble them. Though tart, the berries are fine for jelly or juice (most people prefer their aronia juice blended with other fruits); they've also been used as a dye and food coloring. Recent research reveals that the berries contain abundant phytonutrients—the highest levels ever measured in a fruit—as well as compounds that lower blood sugar and improve insulin production. 'Nero', a good European cultivar, is available.

Cranberry (*Vaccinium macrocarpon*; zones 2 to 6). Gardeners can grow this plant as an edible evergreen groundcover. Though native to acidic bogs, cranberry can be raised in consistently moist, acidic soil (try a raised bed loaded up with a well-drained mix dominated by dampened peat moss). It sends out runners that root at the nodes, so plants spaced 12 inches (30 cm) or so apart will soon fill in and form a handsome mat of small green leaves. Plants are self-pollinizers; the flowers are whitish to pink, followed by red berries in the fall. Cranberry cultivars have been mixed up over the years; it's hard to tell some of them apart, but 'Stevens' is usually an excellent choice. No, you don't need to flood your planting to harvest, like the big cranberry producers do; just pick them right off the stems. Interesting little factoid: quality ripe cranberries bounce; soft, bruised ones do not.

Huckleberry (*Vaccinium membranaceum*, *V. ovatum*, and others; zones 5 to 8). The many native North American species of *Vaccinium* commonly known as huckleberries all pretty much look like a blueberry but may be red, black, or blue in color. They

Huckleberry

Huckleberry

Jostaberry

Jostaberry

are still extensively harvested from wild stands in the Pacific Northwest, much as the lowbush blueberry is in New England and the Canadian Maritimes; famously the "huckleberry handshake" made in the berry fields near Mount Adams (in Washington state) between the Yakama Nation and the National Forest Service set aside areas for Native Americans to pick. This agreement is honored to this day.

The most commonly harvested species, *Vaccinium membranaceum* and *V. deliciosum*, bear luscious, tart berries that are commonly processed since they tear from the plant when picked and therefore have no shelf life. All the more reason to grow these delicious berries yourself! The evergreen huckleberry (*V. ovatum*) not only has abundant sweet fruit but is an outstanding ornamental with small dark green leaves year-round and brilliant red growth in the spring, followed by dainty clusters of pink urn-shaped flowers on a medium-sized shrub; 'Native Star' and 'Thunderbird' are two particularly attractive selections.

Jostaberry (*Ribes* ×*nidigrolaria*; zones [3]4 to 8). This is a hybrid between gooseberry and black currant, with cultural needs and appearance similar to both. It is self-pollinating and produces black fruits about ½ inch (1 cm) in diameter. They are sweeter than gooseberries and very high in vitamin C. Birds love them. The shrubs are extremely cold-hardy and reach 4 to 8 feet (1.2 to 2.5 m) at maturity. Best of all, the plant is thornless and resistant to white pine blister rust. Cultivars include 'Orus 8', 'Red Josta', and 'Jogranda' ('Jostagranda').

Juneberry

Juneberry

Juneberry (*Amelanchier* spp.; zones [3]4 to 9). Ultimately a large multi-stemmed shrub or small tree, *Amelanchier* species are fairly similar and go by a variety of common names in addition to Juneberry, including serviceberry, shadbush, and mountain blueberry. Juneberries are decidedly hardier than highbush blueberries and are grown and enjoyed well up into Canada (hence the common name specific to *Amelanchier alnifolia*, saskatoon, and its tasty berries). All do best in damp, acidic ground and are not particular about exposure. A springtime flurry of white flowers gives way to pink, finally red to purplish black berries in early summer. Fall foliage is bright orange to red. Juneberries are technically pomes, like apples or pears, though they remind some people of blueberries in size and flavor. You will have to beat the birds to them. Cultivars, used mostly as attractive and garden-worthy ornamentals, include the classic 'Autumn Brilliance' and 'Princess Diana', both of which can be 20 to 25 feet (6 to7.5 m) high and wide; for something a bit shorter and narrower, look for 'Cole's Select'. Although these have edible fruits, you may want to choose a cultivar specifically for flavor: 'Pembina' and 'Smokey' (both, no surprise, selections of *A. alnifolia*) are rated best for this.

Lingonberry (*Vaccinium vitis-idaea*; zones 2 to 5[6]). Widely grown in Scandinavia, this bright red berry is similar in its culture to blueberries. A short evergreen shrub or mat-former, it tops out at 12 to 18 inches (30 to 45 cm) high and spreads via underground runners. Particularly dwarf forms (subsp. *minus*) are intriguing. Lingonberry flowers in May and again in August; in some cultivars, like 'Koralle' and 'Ida', fruit ripens in two crops. Plants are self-pollinating, but if you can track down different ones, you can get slightly earlier and larger berries. The tart berries, a bit smaller than cranberries, make a delicious sauce or jam.

Lingonberry

Lingonberry

PERHAPS WE'VE VAGUELY heard of some worrisome ban, or glimpsed a jar of gooseberry jam at a specialty market, or noticed that currant juice is standard on grocery shelves in England. But for most North American gardeners, even the most major of the minor specialty berries simply haven't been on our radar. This is a shame, for gooseberries and currants, of all colors, generate bountiful harvests for minimal work. There are creative, tasty ways to use them in the kitchen, from jellies to pies, from juice to wine. More and more nurseries that sell fruit plants now offer a range of excellent,

disease-resistant cultivars—perhaps you can be the first in your neighborhood to raise and enjoy these delicious specialty berries!

Elderberries are already prized by birdwatchers and those who value the healthful qualities of the berries. But they too deserve more attention. Because the American and European species are so variable, there are many wonderful choices, some especially fruitful, some especially ornamental. They are naturally tough and easy to grow. With all these things going for them, isn't it high time you considered adding a few to your landscape?

RECOMMENDED CULTIVARS BY REGION

The cultivars listed here—described in more detail in the preceding chapters, as well as in the catalogs and websites of the nurseries that offer them—are recommendations only. Local conditions and the care you give your plants will affect performance. Obviously, these lists are not exhaustive—many other cultivars may interest you. So consider these a starting point, and make your choices according to what appeals to you and what is available when you're ready to plant. More cultivars are hitting the market every season.

KEY TO REGIONS

NE = Northeast, including southern Quebec and southern Ontario
SE = Southeast, including Gulf Coast
MW = Midwest and Great Plains, including adjacent Canadian provinces
RM = Rocky Mountain/Mountain West
NW = Pacific Northwest, including Northern California and British Columbia
SW = Southwest and Southern California

NORTHEAST

Strawberries	Raspberries	Blackberries	Blueberries	Gooseberries	Currants	Elderberries
'Albion'	'Anne'	'Chester Thornless'	'Aurora'	'Amish Red'	'Ben Sarek'	'Adams'
'Allstar'	'Autumn Bliss'	'Doyle's'	'Bluecrop'	'Black Velvet'	'Blanka'	'Johns'
'Annapolis'	'Autumn Britten'	'Everthornless'	'Bluegold'	'Captivator'	'Crandall'	'Nova'
'Cavendish'	'Boyne'	'Illini Hardy'	'Blueray'	'Careless'	'Jonkheer van Tets'	'Samdal'
'Earliglow'	'Brandywine'	'Navaho'	'Burgundy'	'Downing'	'Pink Champagne'	'Scotia'
'Honeoye'	'Bristol'/ 'Munger'	'Ouachita'	'Chandler'	'Hinnonmaki Red'	'Red Lake'	'York'
'Jewel'	'Canby'	'Prime-Jan'	'Darrow'	'Hinnonmaki Yellow'	'Rovada'	
'Kent'	'Caroline'	'Prime-Ark 45'	'Draper'	'Poorman'	'Titania'	
'Ozark Beauty'	'Crimson Giant'	'Triple Crown'	'Duke'	'Tixia'	'Wilder'	
'Seascape'	'Fallgold'		'Elliott'	'Welcome'		
'Sparkle'	'Goldie'		'Jersey'			
'Tribute'	'Heritage'		'Liberty'			
'Tristar'	'Jewel'		'Northblue'			
	'Killarney'		'Northland'			
	'Latham'		'Northsky'			
	'Nova'		'Patriot'			
	'Prelude'		'Polaris'			
	'Royalty'		'Spartan'			
	'Taylor'		'Top Hat'			
	'Titan'					

SOUTHEAST

Strawberries
'Albion'
'Chandler'
'Seascape'
'Sequoia'
'Strawberry
Festival'
'Sweet
Charlie'

Raspberries
'Caroline'
'Dormanred'
'Heritage'
'Tulameen'

Blackberries
Most black-
berries should
perform well
in the South-
east.

Blueberries
'Bluebelle'
'Climax'
'Coville'
'Duke'
'Emerald'
'Jewel'
'Jubilee'
'Misty'
'O'Neal'
'Premier'
'Sharpblue'
'Sunshine
Blue'
'Tifblue'
'Vernon'

Gooseberries
No gooseber-
ries are rec-
ommended
for the South-
east.

Currants
No currants
are recom-
mended for
the South-
east.

Elderberries
'Adams'
'Johns'
'Nova'
'Samdal'
'Scotia'
'York'

MIDWEST

Strawberries	Raspberries	Blackberries	Blueberries	Gooseberries	Currants	Elderberries
'Albion'	'Anne'	'Chester Thornless'	'Bluecrop'	'Amish Red'	'Ben Lomond'	'Adams'
'Allstar'	'Autumn Bliss'	'Doyle's'	'Bluegold'	'Black Velvet'	'Ben Sarek'	'Bob Gordon'
'Annapolis'	'Autumn Britten'	'Everthornless'	'Bluejay'	'Captivator'	'Blanka'	'Johns'
'Earliglow'	'Brandywine'	'Hull Thornless'	'Blueray'	'Glenndale'	'Crandall'	'Nova'
'Honeoye'	'Bristol'/ 'Munger'	'Kiowa'	'Bluetta'	'Hinnonmaki Red'	'Jonkheer van Tets'	'Samdal'
'Jewel'	'Canby'	'Natchez'	'Burgundy'	'Hinnonmaki Yellow'	'Pink Champagne'	'Scotia'
'Kent'	'Caroline'	'Navaho'	'Chandler'	'Poorman'	'Red Lake'	'Wyldewood'
'Ogallala'	'Crimson Giant'	'Osage'	'Chippewa'	'Tixia'	'Rovada'	'York'
'Ozark Beauty'	'Fallgold'	'Ouachita'	'Coville'	'Welcome'	'Titania'	
'Seascape'	'Goldie'	'Prime-Jan'	'Darrow'		'Wilder'	
'Sparkle'	'Heritage'	'Prime-Ark 45'	'Draper'			
'Tristar'	'Honey Queen'	'Prime-Ark Freedom'	'Duke'			
	'Jewel'	'Triple Crown'	'Elliott'			
	'Latham'		'Jersey'			
	'Nova'		'Jubilee'			
	'Prelude'		'Legacy'			
	'Royalty'		'Liberty'			
	'Taylor'		'Misty'			
	'Titan'		'Northblue'			
			'Northcountry'			
			'Northland'			
			'Northsky'			
			'Patriot'			
			'Polaris'			
			'Rubel'			
			'Spartan'			
			'Star'			
			'Top Hat'			

ROCKY MOUNTAIN

Strawberries	Raspberries	Blackberries	Blueberries	Gooseberries	Currants	Elderberries
'Albion'	'Anne'	'Illini Hardy'	'Earliblue'	'Downing'	'Ben Lomond'	'Adams'
'Fort Laramie'	'Autumn Britten'	'Prime-Jan'	'Jersey'	'Glenndale'	'Ben Sarek'	'Johns'
'Honeoye'	'Boyne'		'Northblue'	'Invicta'	'Jonkheer van Tets'	'Nova'
'Jewel'	'Brandywine'		'Northcountry'	'Oregon Champion'	'Red Lake'	'Samdal'
'Ogallala'	'Canby'		'Northland'	'Poorman'	'Titania'	'Scotia'
'Seascape'	'Caroline'		'Patriot'	'Red Jacket'	'Wilder'	'York'
'Sequoia'	'Heritage'		'Polaris'	'Welcome'		
'Tribute'	'Honey Queen'					
'Tristar'	'Jewel'					
	'Nova'					
	'Royalty'					

Strawberries
'Albion'
'Benton'
'Honeoye'
'Hood'
'Monterey'
'Portola'
'Puget Reli-
 ance'
'Quinault'
'San Andreas'
'Seascape'
'Shuksan'
'Sweet Sun-
 rise'
'Tillamook'
'Totem'
'Tribute'
'Tristar'

Raspberries
'Amity'
'Anne'
'Autumn Bliss'
'Autumn Brit-
 ten'
'Boyne'
'Brandywine'
'Bristol'/
 'Munger'
'Canby'
'Caroline'
'Cascade
 Bounty'
'Cascade
 Delight'
'Cascade
 Gold'
'Chemainus'
'Heritage'
'Jewel'
'Killarney'
'Latham'
'MacBlack'
'Malahat'
'Meeker'
'Polka'
'Prelude'
'Royalty'
'Saanich'
'Tulameen'
'Vintage'
'Willamette'

Blackberries
'Black
 Diamond'
'Boysen'
'Chester
 Thornless'
'Columbia
 Star'
'Everthorn-
 less'
'Logan'
'Marion'
'Navaho'
'Obsidian'
'Ollalie'
'Ouachita'
'Triple Crown'

Blueberries
'Aurora'
'Bluecrop'
'Bluegold'
'Bluejay'
'Chandler'
'Chippewa'
'Draper'
'Duke'
'Hardyblue'
'Jersey'
'Legacy'
'Liberty'
'Northblue'
'North-
 country'
'Northsky'
'Ochlockonee'
'Perpetua'
'Pink Lemon-
 ade'
'Polaris'
'Powderblue'
'Rubel'
'Spartan'
'Sunshine
 Blue'
'Vernon'

Gooseberries
All goose-
berries should
perform well
in the Pacific
Northwest.

Currants
All currants
should per-
form well in
the Pacific
Northwest.

Elderberries
'Adams'
'Johns'
'Scotia'
'York'

SOUTHWEST

Strawberries
'Albion'
'Camarosa'
'Chandler'
'Monterey'
'Portola'
'San Andreas'
'Seascape'
'Sequoia'
'Strawberry
 Festival'

Raspberries
'Anne'
'Bababerry'
'Brandywine'
'Bristol'/
 'Munger'
'Caroline'
'Heritage'
'Josephine'
'Polana'
'Royalty'

Blackberries
'Black Dia-
 mond'
'Boysen'
'Chester
 Thornless'
'Columbia
 Star'
'Doyle's'
'Everthorn-
 less'
'Hull Thorn-
 less'
'Logan'
'Marion'
'Obsidian'
'Ollalie'
'Prime-Ark 45'
'Triple Crown'

Blueberries
'Bluecrop'
'Climax'
'Draper'
'Duke'
'Jewel'
'Legacy'
'Liberty'
'Ochlockonee'
'Pink Lemon-
 ade'
'Powderblue'
'Spartan'
'Sunshine
 Blue'
'Vernon'

Gooseberries
No gooseber-
ries are rec-
ommended
for the South-
west.

Currants
'Crandall'

Elderberries
No elderber-
ries are rec-
ommended
for the South-
west.

FURTHER READING AND RESOURCES

Books

Carey, Nora, and Michael Hales. 1995. *Perfect Preserves*. New York: Stewart, Tabori & Chang.

Damrosch, Barbara. 2008. *The Garden Primer*. New York: Workman Publishing.

Fall Creek Farm & Nursery. 2011. *A Gardener's Guide to Blueberries*. Lowell, Oregon: Fall Creek Farm & Nursery.

Reich, Lee. 2004. *Uncommon Fruits for Every Garden*. Portland, Oregon: Timber Press.

——. 2010. *The Pruning Book*. 2d ed. Newtown, Connecticut: Taunton Press.

Ridge, Brent, and Josh Kilmer-Purcell, with Sandy Gluck. 2011. *The Beekman 1802 Heirloom Cookbook*. New York: Sterling Epicure.

Websites

backyardberryplants.com
A wonderful berry nursery in Indiana; even if you don't order plants from them, the site is loaded with useful, savvy information on planting and caring for these plants.

extension.oregonstate.edu/gardening/how-choose-and-grow-best-varieties-small-fruits
Updated information and retail nursery sources. Especially good for West Coast gardeners.

fruit.cornell.edu/berry/
Updated information and retail nursery sources; organic guides; pest diagnostic tool and management guidelines; webinars on growing berries. Especially good for East Coast gardeners.

gardening.cornell.edu/fruit/homefruit.html
Good for home gardeners looking to establish a fruit planting at home.

homeorchardsociety.org
A resource for "growing good fruit at home." Articles, forums, other resources, tips, and more. Berries of all kinds (as well as tree fruits).

palspublishing.cals.cornell.edu/
Production guides for the Northeast, Midwest, and eastern Canada: blackberries and raspberries, blueberries, strawberries.

Plant sources

pickyourown.org
A list of pick-your-own farms around the United States, which you may find helpful as you research varieties and flavors before deciding which berries to grow at home. Also plentiful practical information on making preserves, juices, and more from your harvest.

Backyard Berry Plants
backyardberryplants.com

Forestfarm at Pacifica
forestfarm.com

Indiana Berry & Plant Co.
indianaberry.com

Nourse Farms
noursefarms.com

pubs.ext.vt.edu/438/438-107/438-107_pdf. pdf
Specialty Crop Profile: *Ribes* (Gooseberries and Currants), Virginia Cooperative Extension.

One Green World
onegreenworld.com

Raintree Nursery
raintreenursery.com

rosalindcreasy.com
Inspiring and informative website by the acclaimed edible-landscaping pioneer and author.

Sakuma Brothers Farms
sakumabros.com

Spooner Farms
spoonerfarms.com

smallfruits.org
Southern Regional Small Fruit Consortium. Sponsored by Clemson Universtiy, North Carolina State University, and the University of Georgia. Information-packed website, especially good for gardeners in the Southeast.

Stark Bro's
starkbros.com

strawberryplants.org
"If it is even remotely related to strawberry plants, you'll find it here."

ACKNOWLEDGMENTS

For expert assistance in the preparation of this book, special thanks to Marvin Pritts of Cornell University's Cooperative Extension Service; Chad Finn, research geneticist at the USDA in Corvallis, Oregon; Richard McGinnis of McGinnis Berry Crops Limited; Mark Bolda, director of the UC Cooperative Extension, Santa Cruz County, California; Patrick Byers, regional horticultural specialist at the University of Missouri's Greene County Cooperative Extension office; and Kim Hummer, research leader and location coordinator, USDA ARS National Clonal Germplasm Repository, Corvallis, Oregon.

Many thanks to Margaret Roach (awaytogarden.com), herbalist Lisa Ferguson Crow, and the staff at Timber Press for their vision, unflagging support, and enthusiasm.

Lastly, thanks to Alan Chace, Tristan Dunn, and Wes Dunn—and to Guy Clark, for stuff that works.

—TERI DUNN CHACE

PHOTOGRAPHY CREDITS

Page 100, Sarah Milhollin
Page 101 (left), Marci LeBrun
Page 101 (right), Sarah Milhollin
Page 102, Sarah Milhollin
Page 103, Marci LeBrun
Page 107 (top), Flickr/Julie Stockdale
Page 107 (bottom), Flickr/Christine Sparks
Page 109, Marci LeBrun
Page 110, iStock/AdShooter
Page 111, GAP/Rob Whitworth
Page 112, GAP/Fiona Lea
Page 114, GAP/Jo Whitworth
Page 117, Sarah Milhollin
Page 118, Sarah Milhollin
Page 120 (left), GAP/Zara Napier
Page 120 (right), GAP/Dave Bevan
Page 123, Flickr/Amy Kay Watson
Page 125, Marci LeBrun
Page 127, Sarah Milhollin
Page 128, Shutterstock/ET1972
Page 130, iStock/Monique Rodriguez
Page 133, Sarah Milhollin
Page 134, Marci LeBrun
Page 135 (left), Marci LeBrun
Page 135 (center and right), Sarah Milhollin
Page 136 (left and center), Marci LeBrun
Page 136 (right), Sarah Milhollin
Page 137, Marci LeBrun
Page 138, GAP/Tim Gainey
Page 140, Flickr/Sarah A. Sturtevant
Page 141, Sarah Milhollin
Page 142, David Fishman
Page 143, Marci LeBrun
Page 145 (left), Sarah Milhollin
Page 145 (right), iStock/visionsofmaine
Page 148, iStock/Wholden
Page 149, Sarah Milhollin
Page 152, iStock/Middelveld
Page 153, Marci LeBrun

Page 155, GAP/Michael Howes
Page 157, iStock/Whiteway
Page 158, GAP/Juliette Wade
Page 159, Flickr/Julia A. Roebuck
Page 160, GAP/Jonathan Buckley
Page 161, GAP/Elke Borkowski
Page 162 (left), GAP/Michael Howes
Page 162 (right), Flickr/Manu
Page 163, GAP/Paul Debois
Page 165 (left), GAP/Tim Gainey
Page 165 (right), GAP/Paul Debois
Page 167 (left), GAP/Paul Debois
Page 167 (center), GAP/John Glover
Page 167 (right), GAP/Michael Howes
Page 168, GAP/Friedrich Strauss
Page 170 (left), Shutterstock/Lakov Filimonov
Page 170 (right), Flickr/Julia A. Roebuck
Page 171, GAP/Dave Bevan
Page 172 (left), GAP/Michael Howes
Page 172 (right), Flickr/Thomas L. Rodebaugh III
Page 173 (left), GAP/S&O
Page 173 (right), GAP/Michael Howes
Page 174 (left), GAP/Michael Howes
Page 174 (right), Shutterstock/Jeanie333
Page 176 (left), iStock/Kokodrill
Page 176 (right), GAP/Howard Rice
Page 177, Wikimedia/Gary Houston
Page 179, iStock/Katra
Page 180, iStock/Mweirauch
Page 181, Wikimedia/Derek Jensen
Page 184 (left), Johanna James
Page 184 (right), Flickr/Wendy Cutler
Page 185 (left), Wikimedia/Meneerke Bloem
Page 185 (right), iStock/SmallFrog
Page 186, Flickr/Willamette Biology
Page 187, Wikimedia/Simon Eugster
Page 188, Johanna James
Page 189 (left), Wikimedia/Algirdas
Page 189 (right), Wikimedia/Jonas Bergsten

INDEX

'Adams', 180
'Albion', 62
'Alexandria', 63
'Allstar', 61
alpine strawberry (*Fragaria vesca*),
    9, 38, 57, 58, 59–60, 63–64
'Amish Red', 164
'Amity', 99
'Annapolis', 61
'Anne', 99
anthracnose (*Colletotrichum* spp.,
    Elsinoë veneta), 80, 120, 121
aphids, 31, 122, 176
'Aurea', 178
'Aurora', 133
'Autumn Bliss', 99
'Autumn Brilliance', 188
'Autumn Britten', 99

'Bababerry', 99
'Ben Lomond', 166
'Ben Sarek', 166, 167
'Benton', 61
bindweed (*Convolvulus* spp.), 64
birds, 8, 83, 84,123–124, 152–153,
    176, 184
'Black Beauty', 178
blackberry (*Rubus* spp.), 9, 87–124
  buying plants, 105, 122
  choosing the right cultivar, 96–97,
    101–103
  fertilizing, 112–113
  hardiness zones, 94
  harvesting, 95, 117–119
  as hedges or living fences, 42, 45,
    87–88
  mulching, 111–112

overwintering, 118
planting, 105–106
pruning, 95, 112, 115–117
ripeness, determining, 118
site selection, 104
soil requirements, 104–105
storage of picked berries, 118–119
suckers and invasiveness, 33, 50,
    88, 90, 114
sunlight requirements, 104
trellis systems, 42, 106–111, 116
troubleshooting, 111–112, 119–124
watering, 112
blackberry, erect, 88, 90, 94–95,
    101–102, 111–112, 115
blackberry, fall-bearing, 88, 95
blackberry, hybrid, 93
blackberry, semi-erect, 88, 90,
    95–96, 102, 115–116
blackberry, thornless, 87, 94, 95,
    96, 101, 102, 103
blackberry, trailing, 7, 88, 90, 96,
    102–103, 116
black chokeberry (*Aronia melano-
    carpa, Photinia melanocarpa*),
    9, 184–185
'Black Diamond', 96, 97, 102
'Black Lace', 178
'Black Velvet', 164
'Blanka', 166–167
'Bluebelle', 137
blueberry (*Vaccinium* spp.), 7, 8, 9,
    16, 38, 43, 125–154, 156
  berry size and flavor, 129–130
  buying plants, 140
  choosing the right cultivar, 132–
    138

blueberry *(continued)*
  in containers, 47, 141–142
  fertilizing, 143, 147
  flowers, 43, 130
  foliage color, 12, 43, 44, 127, 132, 154
  harvesting, 132, 147
  for landscaping, 38, 39, 40, 43, 126, 127, 128
  mulching, 142–143
  overwintering, 148–149
  planting, 140, 141
  pollination, 127, 130–31, 132, 133, 135, 136
  pruning, 131, 144–147
  site selection, 139–140
  soil pH and fertility, 18, 39, 129, 139–140
  storage of picked berries, 147–148
  sunlight requirements, 22, 139
  troubleshooting, 149–154
  watering, 141, 143
blueberry, half-high, 38, 132, 138
blueberry, lowbush (*Vaccinium angustifolium*), 38, 39, 128, 131–132, 137
blueberry, Northern highbush (*Vaccinium corymbosum*), 128, 131, 133–136
blueberry, rabbiteye (*Vaccinium virgatum*), 9, 128, 132, 137–138
blueberry, Southern highbush, 131, 136–137
blueberry maggot (*Rhagoletis mendax*), 150–151
'Bluecrop', 133–134, 146
'Bluegold', 134
'Bluejay', 134
'Blueray', 134, 146
'Bluetta', 134, 146
'Bob Gordon', 181
'Boyne', 97
'Boysen', 97, 102
boysenberry, 88, 91, 93, 96
'Brandywine', 101
'Brazos', 101
'Bristol', 101
'Burgundy', 137

'Camarosa', 61

Canada thistle (*Cirsium arvense*), 64
'Canby', 14, 97
cane blight (*Leptosphaeria coniothyrium*), 120
cankers, 150, 184
'Captivator', 165
'Careless', 165
'Caroline', 100
'Cascade Bounty', 98
'Cascade Delight', 98
'Cascade Gold', 100
'Chandler' (blueberry), 134, 146
'Chandler' (strawberry), 61
'Chemainus', 98
cherry fruitworm (*Grapholita packardi*), 151
'Chester Thornless', 96, 102
Chilean strawberry (*Fragaria chiloensis*), 53, 54
'Chippewa', 138
climate, 13–16. *See also* hardiness zones; *specific berries*
  cultivar selection and, 25, 58, 60
  harvesting times and, 9, 57
  solarizing soil and, 31
  sun/UV damage and, 21
'Climax', 137
'Cole's Select', 188
'Columbia Star', 96, 97, 103
container gardens, 8, 45–47, 70
  blueberries in, 141–142
  raspberries in, 96
  strawberries in, 70–73
Cooperative Extension Service, 13, 17, 25, 60, 96, 133, 164, 175
cover crops, 20–21, 104
'Coville', 134, 146
Coville, Frederick, 129
cranberry (*Vaccinium macrocarpon*), 9, 18, 38, 47, 185
cranberry fruitworm (*Acrobasis vaccinii*), 151
'Crandall', 167
'Crimson Giant', 100
crumbly berry, 28
currants (*Ribes* spp.), 8, 156, 159–162
  buying plants, 169
  choosing the right cultivar, 164, 166–167

drainage, 168
fan-training, 160
fertilizing, 171–172
foliage, 162
fruit size and color, 162, 163
hardiness zones, 163
harvesting, 173, 174
for landscaping, 38
legality of growing, 164
mulching, 170, 171
overwintering, 174
planting, 170
pollination, 163
pruning, 172, 173
shrub size, 160
site selection, 168–169
soil pH and fertility, 169
sunlight requirements, 22, 169
sweetness, determining, 174
troubleshooting, 174–177
watering, 171
white pine blister rust and, 164,
    169, 170, 175
currants, black (*Ribes nigrum*), 9,
    25, 156, 159, 164
currants, clove (*Ribes aureum* var.
    villosum), 159, 164
currants, red (*Ribes rubrum, R.
    sativum, R. petraeum*), 9, 159
currants, white, 9, 159
currant borer (*Synanthedon tipuli-
    formis*), 175
currant fruit fly (*Euphranta
    canadensis*), 176
currant stem girdler (*Janus integer*),
    175

dandelions, 27–28
'Darrow', 134
'Dart's Greenlace', 178
diseases, 26–27, 79. *See also specific
    diseases*
'Dormanred', 98
'Downing', 165
'Doyle's', 102
drainage, 22
    for blackberries and raspberries,
        104
    for container gardens, 73, 141
    for gooseberries and currants, 168
    raised beds and, 23, 69

site selection and, 16, 22
    for strawberries, 64, 65, 69
'Draper', 135
'Duke', 135

'Earliblue', 135, 146
'Earliglow, 61
'Early Sulphur', 165
elderberry (*Sambucus* spp.), 7, 8, 25,
    156, 157, 177–184, 189
    buying plants, 182
    choosing the right cultivar, 180–
        181
    fertilizing, 183
    flowers, 12, 179
    fruit, 43, 179–180
    harvesting, 183
    for landscaping, 38, 43, 157, 178,
        189
    light and soil requirements, 182
    mulching, 182
    overwintering, 183–184
    planting, 182
    pollination, 180, 181, 182
    pruning, 183
    site selection, 181–182
    storage of picked berries, 183
    suckers and invasiveness, 182
    troubleshooting, 184
    watering, 182–183
elder shoot borer (*Desmocerus pal-
    liatus*), 184
'Elliott', 135, 146
'Emerald', 136
'Everthornless', 103
'Explorer', 93–94

'Fallgold'
fertilizer
    for blackberries and raspberries,
        105, 112–113
    for blueberries, 144, 147
    for elderberries, 183
    for gooseberries and currants,
        171–172
    inorganic or chemical, 18
    K (potassium), 16, 18–19, 105, 144
    magnesium, 19
    micronutrients, 19–20
    N (nitrogen), 16, 19, 21, 75, 80,
        104, 105, 112–13

fertilizer (continued)
  organic or natural sources, 18 (see also specific nutrients)
  P (phosphorus), 16, 18, 65, 105
  for strawberries, 65, 72, 75
  sulfur/lime sulfur, 16, 18, 120, 121, 139, 144, 175
floricanes, 94
'Fort Laramie," 63
'Franor', 63
Fuller, Andrew S., 109
fungal diseases, 26, 112, 119–122, 150, 169, 174–175

'Gerald Straley', 63
'Glenndale', 165
'Goldie', 100
gooseberry (Ribes spp.), 156, 157–159, 160, 162–163
  buying plants, 169
  choosing the right cultivar, 163–166
  container gardens and, 47
  drainage, 168
  fertilizing, 171–172
  fruit size and color, 162
  growing on supports, 158
  hardiness zones, 163
  harvesting, 173, 174
  for landscaping, 38, 43, 45
  mulching, 170, 171
  overwintering, 174
  planting, 170
  pollination, 163
  pruning, 172, 173
  shrub size, 160
  site selection, 168–169
  soil pH and fertility, 169
  sunlight requirements, 22, 169
  thorniness, 162, 168, 173, 174
  troubleshooting, 174–177
  watering, 171
gooseberry maggot, 176
gooseberry sawfly (Nematus ribesii), 175
gray mold (Botrytis cinerea), 79–80, 120–121
gypsy moths, 150

hardiness zones, 13–15, 25
'Hardyblue', 135

harvesting
  blackberries and raspberries, 95, 117–118
  blueberries, 132, 147
  currants, 173, 174
  elderberries, 183
  extending or staggering, 9, 60
  gooseberries, 173, 174
  removing fruit rots, 33–34
  ripe fruit, 33
  strawberries, 59, 60, 76
'Heritage', 97, 100
'Hinnonmaki Red', 165
'Hinnonmaki Yellow', 165
'Honeoye', 61
'Honey Queen', 100
'Hood', 61
huckleberry (Vaccinium membranaceum, V. ovatum, and others), 9, 127, 185–187
'Hull Thornless', 102

'Ida', 188
'Illini Hardy', 101
'Invicta', 165

Japanese beetles, 31, 122–123, 150
'Jersey', 133, 135, 146
'Jewel' (blueberry), 136
'Jewel' (raspberry), 101
'Jewel' (strawberry), 61
'Joan J', 96
'Jogranda' ('Jostagranda'), 187
'Johns', 181
Johnson grass (Sorghum halepense), 64
'Jonkheer van Tets', 167
'Josephine', 100
jostaberry (Ribes ×nidigrolaria), 9, 187
'Jubilee', 136
Juneberry (Amelanchier spp.), 9, 38, 188

'Killarney', 98
'Kiowa', 101
'Koralle', 188

'Laciniata', 178
landscaping with berries, 7, 10, 12, 36–50

berry plant forms, 38
blackberries or raspberries, 42, 45,
    87–88
blueberries, 38, 39, 40, 43, 126,
    127, 128
as container displays, 45–47
creative supports and, 42
crop maintenance and, 48, 50
currant bush, 37
elderberries, 38, 43, 157, 178, 189
gooseberries, 38, 43, 45
as groundcovers and edgings, 7,
    38–39, 42, 47, 53, 54, 59, 63,
    128
as hedges or living fences, 42–45,
    87–88, 106
huckleberry, 187
Juneberry, 188
as ornamentals, 7, 10, 12, 22, 37,
    38, 53, 54, 59, 63, 126, 138, 157,
    178, 187, 188, 189
pitfalls of, 48–50
shady conditions and, 22
strawberries, 41, 53, 54, 59, 63
'Langley Gage', 165
'Latham', 98
leather rot (Phytophthora cactorum),
    80
'Legacy', 133, 135
'Liberty', 135
lingonberry (Vaccinium vitis-idaea),
    9, 18, 38, 39, 188–189
'Lipstick', 63
'Loch Ness', 96
'Logan', 93, 103
loganberry, 88, 91, 93, 96

'MacBlack', 101
'Malahat', 98
'Marion', 93, 97, 103
marionberry, 103
marsh cinquefoil (Comarum palus-
    tre), 63
'Maxima', 178
'Meeker', 98
'Mignonette', 63
'Misty', 136
mites, 28–29, 31
'Monterey', 62
mountain blueberry. See Juneberry
mulch

for blackberries and raspberries,
    111–112
for blueberries, 142–143, 153–154
for elderberries, 182
for gooseberries and currants,
    170, 171
leaf mulch caution, 143
recommended kinds, 73, 111, 143,
    154, 170
soil-borne fungal diseases and, 112
for strawberries, 73, 78
mummy berry (Monilinia vac-
    cinii-corymbosii), 150
'Munger', 101

'Natchez', 96, 101
'Native Star', 187
'Navaho', 96, 97, 101
nematodes, 27, 122
'Nero', 185
'Newberry', 93
'Niwot', 93–94
'Northblue', 138
'Northcountry', 138
'Northland', 138
'Northsky', 138
'Nova', 98, 181
nutgrass (Cyperus rotundus), 64

'Obsidian', 103
'Ochlockonee', 137
'Ogallala', 63
'Olallie' (blackberry), 103
'Olallie' (raspberry), 94
'O'Neal', 136
'Oregon Champion', 166
'Orus 8', 187
'Osage', 102
'Ouachita', 96, 97, 102
'Ozark Beauty', 63

'Patriot', 136
'Pembina', 188
'Perpetua', 138
pest control, 12, 29–34
    Bt (Bacillus thuringiensis), 150,
        151, 175
    milky spore, 123
    solarizing the soil, 31, 104
pests, 28–29, 31, 83. See also specific
    pests

phytophthora root rot (*Phytoph-thora fragariae* var. *rubi*), 121
'Pink Champagne', 167
'Pink Lemonade', 137
'Pink Panda', 63
'Plena', 178
'Polana', 100
'Polaris', 138
pollination
    blueberries, 127, 130–31, 132, 133, 135, 136
    currants, 163
    elderberries, 180, 181, 182
    frost and inhibiting, 14
    gooseberries, 163
    insecticide caution, 34
    strawberries, 56
'Polka', 100
'Poorman', 166
'Portola', 63
'Powderblue', 137
powdery mildew (*Podosphaera aphanis*), 80, 175
'Prelude', 98
'Premier', 137
'Prime-Ark 45', 88, 102
'Prime-Ark Freedom', 102
'Prime-Jan', 102
primocanes, 94
'Princess Diana', 188
Pritts, Marvin, 83
pruning, 12, 33
    blackberries, trailing, 115–116
    blackberries, erect, 115
    blackberries, semi-erect, 115–116
    blueberries, 144–147
    elderberries, 183
    gooseberries and currants, 172
    raspberries, black and purple, 115
    raspberries, fall-bearing red, 114–115
    raspberries, summer-bearing red, 113–114
'Puget Reliance', 61–62

quackgrass (*Elymus repens*), 64
'Quinault', 63

rain gauge, 16
raised beds, 22–24
    for cranberries, 185
    for raspberries, 104, 121
    for strawberries, 58, 65, 68–70, 79
raspberry (*Rubus* spp.), 86–124
    buying plants, 105, 122
    choosing the right cultivar, 14, 96–101
    fertilizing, 112–113
    hardiness zones and, 14
    harvesting, 95, 117–119
    as hedges or living fences, 42, 87–88, 106
    mulching, 111–112
    overwintering, 119
    planting, 105–107
    pruning, 93, 112–115, 116–117
    "rat tails," 93
    ripeness, determining, 117–118
    site selection, 104
    soil requirements, 104–105
    storage of picked berries, 118–119
    suckers and invasiveness, 33, 50, 88, 90, 106, 114
    sunlight requirements, 104
    trellis systems, 42, 106–111
    troubleshooting, 119–124
    UV damage and, 21, 124
    watering, 112
    yields, 86
raspberry, black (*Rubus occidentalis*), 9, 90, 91, 93–94, 97, 101, 104, 115
raspberry, fall-bearing, 87, 88, 93–94, 99–101, 114
raspberry, purple, 9, 89, 90, 94, 101, 115
raspberry, red (*Rubus idaeus*), 9, 50, 86, 87, 88, 89, 90, 91, 97, 104, 106, 111, 113–115
raspberry, summer-bearing, 87, 97–99
raspberry, thornless, 96
raspberry, yellow- to gold-fruited, 91, 92
raspberry bushy dwarf virus, 122
'Raspberry Shortcake', 96
'Red Jacket', 166
'Red Josta', 187
'Red Lake', 167
red stele (*Phytophthora fragariae*), 80
'Rosea Plena', 178

'Rovada', 167
'Royalty', 101
'Rubel', 129, 136
'Ruby Red', 63
'Rugen Improved', 64

'Samdal', 181
'San Andreas', 63
sap beetles (*Stelidota geminata*), 31, 82
'Scotia', 181
'Seascape', 63
sedges (*Carex* spp.), 64
'Sequoia', 62
serviceberry. *See* Juneberry
shadbush. *See* Juneberry
'Sharpblue', 136
'Shuksan', 62
site selection, 13–16
   for blackberries and raspberries, 104
   for blueberries, 139–140
   cultivar choice and, 25–26
   drainage, 22
   for elderberries, 181–182
   for gooseberries and currants, 168–169
   pest control and, 31
   raised beds, 22–24
   soil fertility concerns, 16–21
   for strawberries, 64
   sunlight analysis, 21–22
slugs and snails, 28, 31, 70, 83
Small Fruit Culturist, The (Fuller), 109
'Smokey', 188
soil fertility and pH, 16–21. *See also* fertilizers
   amending pH, 18, 139, 144, 147
   for blackberries and raspberries, 104–105
   for blueberries, 18, 39, 129, 139–140
   for currants, 169
   for elderberries, 182
   for gooseberries, 169
   for strawberries, 38–39, 64–65
soil tests, 17, 20
'Sparkle', 62
'Spartan', 133, 136

spotted wing drosophila (*Drosophila suzukii*), 82–83, 123, 151–152
'Star', 136
'Stevens', 185
storage of picked berries
   blackberries and raspberries, 118–119
   blueberries, 147–148
   elderberries, 183
   strawberries, 76
strawberry (*Fragaria ×ananassa*), 7, 9, 52–84. *See also* alpine strawberry
   buying plants, 65–66
   choosing the right cultivar, 54, 60–64
   in containers, 46, 47, 70–73
   crop maintenance, 50
   drainage and, 55, 65
   fertilizers for, 65, 72, 75
   frost damage, 64, 77–78
   fruit size, 56
   as groundcovers and edgings, 38, 41, 53, 54, 59, 63
   harvesting, 59, 60, 76
   longevity of patch, 75
   mounded beds for, 22–23, 55
   mulching, 73, 74
   as ornamentals, 63
   overwintering, 77–78
   pinching, 76
   planting, 33, 65, 66–72
   pollination, 56
   runners and invasiveness, 50, 55
   quasi-dormancy, 50
   raised beds and, 58, 65, 68–70, 79
   renovation of beds, 76–77
   site choice, 64
   soil fertility and pH, 38, 65, 70
   storage of picked berries, 76
   sunlight requirements, 64–65
   troubleshooting, 54, 78–84
   watering, 73–75
strawberry, day-neutral, 57–58, 59, 60, 62–63, 75
strawberry, everbearing, 57, 58–59, 63
strawberry, June-bearing (short-day), 57, 59, 60, 61–62, 67, 70, 75, 76–77

strawberry clipper or strawberry bud weevil (*Anthonomus signatus*), 82
'Strawberry Festival', 62
strawberry leaf spot (*Mycosphaerella fragariae*), 80
strawberry root weevil (*Otiorhynchus ovatus*), 82
sunlight, 21–22
    for blackberries and raspberries, 104
    for blueberries, 22, 139
    for currants and gooseberries, 169
    for elderberries, 182
    solarizing the soil, 31, 104
    for strawberries, 64
    UV damage and, 21, 124
'Sunshine Blue', 137
'Sutherland Gold', 178
'Sweet Charlie', 62
'Sweet Sunrise', 62

tarnished plant bug (*Lygus* spp.), 29, 81
tayberry, 88, 93
'Taylor', 99
'Thornless Logan', 103
'Thunderbird', 187
'Tifblue', 137
'Tillamook', 62
'Titan', 97, 99
'Titania', 167
'Tixia' ('Rafzicta'), 166
tobacco ringspot virus, 27–28
tomato ringspot virus, 184
'Top Hat', 138
'Totem', 62
trellises and supports
    for blackberries and raspberries, 106–111, 116
    for gooseberries, 158
    "T" (or horizontal) system, 110, 111
'Tribute', 63

'Triple Crown', 96, 97, 102
'Tristar', 63
'Tulameen', 14, 99

verticillium wilt (*Verticillium* spp.), 80, 104
viruses, 26, 121–122
'Vernon', 138
'Vintage', 101

watering
    blackberries and raspberries, 112
    blueberries, 141, 143
    currants and gooseberries, 171
    elderberries, 182–183
    in-ground irrigation system, 34, 112
    at ground level, 30, 31, 112
    soaker hose for, 31, 74, 112, 143
    strawberries, 73–75
weeds, 12, 27–28, 33
    blackberries or raspberries and, 111–112, 122
    blueberries and, 153–154
    currants or gooseberries and, 176–177
    elderberries and, 184
    mulching for control, 33, 73, 111, 142, 153–154, 170, 182
    strawberries and, 64, 83–84
'Welcome', 166
western dewberry (*Rubus ursinus*), 93
'Whinham's Industry', 166
White, Elizabeth, 128–129
white pine blister rust (*Cronartium ribicola*), 164, 169, 174–175, 187
'Wilder', 167
'Willamette', 14, 99
'Wyldewood', 181

'Yellow Wonder', 64
'York', 181